RHYTHM MAN

The Michigan American Music Series

Richard Crawford, Series General Editor

The Michigan American Music Series focuses on leading
figures of American jazz and popular music, assessing both
the uniqueness of their work and its place in the context of
American musical tradition.

Jazz from the Beginning
    By Garvin Bushell as Told to Mark Tucker

Twenty Years on Wheels
    By Andy Kirk as Told to Amy Lee

The Song of the Hawk: The Life and Recordings of Coleman Hawkins
    By John Chilton

Boy Meets Horn
    By Rex Stewart; edited by Claire P. Gordon

Rhythm Man: Fifty Years in Jazz
    By Steve Jordan with Tom Scanlan

Sondheim's Broadway Musicals
    By Stephen Banfield

RHYTHM MAN

Fifty Years in Jazz

Steve Jordan

with Tom Scanlan

Ann Arbor

THE UNIVERSITY OF MICHIGAN PRESS

First paperback edition 1993
Copyright © by the University of Michigan 1991
All rights reserved
Published in the United States of America by
The University of Michigan Press
Manufactured in the United States of America

1994 1993   4   3   2

Library of Congress Cataloging-in-Publication Data

Jordan, Steve, 1919–
    Rhythm man : fifty years in jazz / Steve Jordan, with Tom Scanlan.
       p.   cm. — (The Michigan American music series)
    "Selected discography": p.
    Includes index.
    ISBN 0-472-10256-7 (cloth : alk. paper) — ISBN 0-472-08202-7 (paper : alk. paper)
    1. Jordan, Steve, 1919– . 2. Jazz musicians—United States—
Biography. I. Scanlan, Tom. II. Title. III. Series.
ML419.J73A3   1991
787.87′165′092—dc20
[B]   91-28473
                                        CIP

For all the girls I've known and loved,
especially my two permanent ones,
Patty and Julie

CONTENTS

INTRODUCTION

Tom Scanlan

It's tragic. What Steve does he does better than anyone else in the world! But there's no market for it!
—Drummer Barrett Deems, between sets at the 1980 Manassas Jazz Festival.

Stephen Philip Jordan, born in New York City on January 15, 1919, is a musician's musician and one of the best rhythm guitar players in jazz history. Thinking of all the many electric guitar soloists better known to the public than acoustic guitarist Jordan, clarinetist Peanuts Hucko had it right when he summed up Jordan to me as "a diamond in a field of imitation gold."

Rhythm master Jordan, who can also play marvelous solos, using chords rather than single-note lines, is certainly not a "famous" player to the nation's jazz audience. For decades now, the "famous" and "major" jazz guitarists have been those who play amplified guitar, using their electrified instruments as a "horn," usually playing one note at a time.

Freddie Green is probably the only rhythm guitar player, living or dead, most younger jazz enthusiasts can name. Green was a wonderful player with a distinctive sound who made the Basie band *sound* like the Basie band more than any other Basie band member save the Count himself. But if Green had not been with Basie from 1937 until Basie's death in 1984 (indeed, Freddie was still playing with the Count-less Basie band the night he died at age seventy-five in 1987), Green would be, like Jordan, a great player known only to those inside the world of jazz. (Incidentally, Basie's major advice to new sidemen coming into his band was, for good reason, "listen to the guitar player!")

This is not to suggest that Jordan plays like Green. Green played like Green. Jordan plays like Jordan. Though both were schooled in the George Van Eps fingering system as taught by Allan Reuss, Jordan's sound is tighter and can be more walloping, Green's softer and deeper. This is due partly to their instruments of choice, partly to their action (distance of the strings from the fingerboard), and partly to the way they think rhythm guitar should sound. On a 1954 Buck Clayton all-star "jam session" LP on Columbia (*Jumpin' at the Woodside*), where tricky splicing of two recording dates has Steve in the rhythm section for one part and Freddie for another part of the same track on the LP, the difference in their sounds is plain. Who's better, Green or Jordan? It's a matter of taste.

And, as few know, Steve Jordan was the first guitarist to be offered Freddie Green's chair in the Count Basie band after Freddie died between sets in Las Vegas in 1987. Steve had three days to consider the offer, which meant joining the band in California. Steve says he was "proud of being first call" for Freddie's job, one Green had with Basie for fifty years, and would have enjoyed playing in the swinging Basie band (a band, if you are wondering, that has had more than a few white players in recent decades, a kind of reverse integration you might say). But Steve had to turn the job down because, at age sixty-eight, he simply did not want to return to the road and travel to all those one-nighters the Basie band plays.

Rhythm is the blood and bone of jazz, and unamplified rhythm guitar has certainly been an important sound in jazz and American dance music. But rhythm guitarists, now a dying breed, have usually been ignored by most jazz historians, critics, and journalists. Few who have written about jazz begin to understand the tough, sophisticated art of playing rhythm guitar the right way. Many amplified guitar soloists don't know much about rhythm guitar either. I watched the late Wes Montgomery, one of the greatest of all jazz guitar soloists, study Jordan's left hand playing chords. He was clearly impressed, and when Steve left the bandstand he told Steve, "It sounds great, but I don't understand what you're doing!" And I'm sure he didn't.

Rhythm guitar requires special harmonic knowledge—you must know how to voice chords properly—and it is not easily learned. You cannot learn how to play rhythm from a guitar chord book. Nor can you learn how by studying records. And, as George Van Eps has said, "There are very few six-string chords that can be played in any kind of continuity that makes any kind of sense. Eliminating double notes clarifies the sound." Rhythm guitar is a complicated art.

The jazz world is understandably proud of many electric guitar players who have followed in the giant footsteps of Charlie Christian, who died in 1942 at age twenty-three as he was creating an exciting, major new jazz solo sound with the Benny Goodman Sextet. But Charlie didn't play rhythm well enough to handle that job properly in a Goodman big band (when Christian was with Benny, Mike Bryan was usually the rhythm guitarist in the band). Christian disciples soon multiplied and young rhythm guitar players became extremely rare. After all, the money was up front, in the solo spotlight.

Steve has meaningful things to say about his way of playing guitar in this book. But this book isn't about guitar playing. Also, unlike most memoirs of jazz musicians, it isn't primarily about himself. Perhaps because he is modest by nature, or is accustomed to being—usually—in the background on stage, not in the solo spotlight, this book is mainly about other musicians. And few jazz players still with us have worked with such a variety of famous and obscure jazz characters.

Steve's professional career began during the swing era, also the big band era. By age twenty he was on the road with the Will Bradley–Ray McKinley band. He was with the last band led by Artie Shaw before Shaw entered the Navy during World War II, and with Teddy Powell's underrated band. And after the World War II years in a Navy dance band led by Saxie Dowell, Jordan saw further big band service with Bob Chester, Freddie Slack, Glen Gray, Stan Kenton, and Boyd Raeburn, among others. He also worked in Benny Goodman big bands and sextets off and on for four years during the 1950s. Many fine musicians worked for both Goodman and Shaw, but who else but Steve Jordan has worked for Goodman, Shaw, Stan Kenton, and Boyd Raeburn?

Jazz discographers can tell you that *Steve Jordan, guitar* is on many recordings with the great and near-great of jazz. He has recorded with Vic Dickenson, Mel Powell, Buck Clayton, Ruby Braff, Edmond Hall, Gene Krupa, Coleman Hawkins, Roy Eldridge, Buddy Tate, Jimmy Rushing, and many other prominent jazz players. In nightclubs, his guitar has given harmonic support and rhythmic push to the solo artistry of Pee Wee Russell, Charlie Shavers, Red Allen, Bud Freeman, Billy Butterfield, Wild Bill Davison, Bobby Hackett, and other honored jazz heroes. Standout singers such as the late Maxine Sullivan, Lurlean Hunter, and Helen Ward have been quick to praise his skill as an accompanist.

Steve is quite a singer, too. During thirty years of playing and singing in nightclubs in the Washington, D.C., area, he has had many loyal fans ask him to sing one more.

Jordan specializes in singing old tunes seldom heard today such as *It Happened in Monterey, I Go for That, At Sundown, Last Night on the Back Porch, Nina Never Knew, Tangerine, Fools Rush In, Cuckoo in the Clock,* and *You're Driving Me Crazy.* Among the many admirers of Jordan's singing was the unforgettable Pee Wee Russell. "Just listen to that marvelous phrasing," he told me one night as we sat at a table in Washington's Blues Alley club listening to Steve do his solo turn, accompanied only by his own guitar.

Steve stopped singing in public after a 1982 throat cancer operation and subsequent radiation treatments that left the timbre of his voice diminished. Though many of us would rather hear Steve sing, even with less timbre, than listen to most other singers with full tenor voices intact, he didn't like the way he sounded. But by 1988 his voice was much stronger and he began to sing in public again. Today, those unaware of Steve's throat operation would not guess that he had ever had one listening to him talk. Or sing.

And since some jazz today understandably strikes many, young and old, as mysterious, arty, and often angry music full of odd sounds and squeaks signifying who knows what, younger readers are forewarned that Steve and the jazz musicians he writes about are a different breed of cat in a different field of activity.

Steve's generation of jazz musicians liked and played songs. Although the jazz spirit inspired them to embellish and stray from a given melodic line, a song's melody was kept somewhere in mind. Most any Benny Goodman, Lester Young, or Roy Eldridge improvisation on a song by Irving Berlin, George Gershwin, Cole Porter, whomever, will prove this point. A song's chord pattern, even when augmented or altered for added interest or challenge, kept the swing era players from swinging helter-skelter, minus any kind of musical discipline, into the wild blue yonder.

Jazz as Steve Jordan and his swing era colleagues knew it, was joyful music, primarily, and they never thought or pretended to think that their music somehow rivaled Beethoven for profundity. Jazz was a form of self-expression, to be sure, but it was also playing *with* and *for* others. Also, playing for dancers wasn't viewed as distasteful. I have known many swing era musicians who preferred to watch dancers move to their music than to watch people staring at them from seats in a concert hall.

As suggested earlier, this book is not an autobiography. Much about Steve's more than fifty years in music is here but there is little about his personal life. He mentions one serious youthful romance, with a big band singer, but offers no details. I think he feels his personal life is his own business and wouldn't interest readers anyway. In any event, that's how he wanted this book to be. For the record, however, Steve was a bachelor during his years on the road in big bands. But after moving from New York City to Washington, D.C., in 1959, he met and married, in 1963, his one and only bride Pat, daughter of prominent Scripps-Howard newspaperman Dan Kidney. Pat is well known and highly respected in Washington advertising circles for her newspaper advertising work. Steve also has a loving stepdaughter, Julie. Pat and Steve live in Alexandria, Virginia, across the Potomac River from Washington.

Steve is an expert on men's clothes (John Hammond told me that Steve knows as much about clothes as George Frazier does!) and has worked in clothing stores when music jobs were scarce. In fact, that's why he moved to Washington. There were few gigs or recording dates for a rhythm guitar player in New York in 1959, and most all of the remaining big bands had dropped guitar to save money. A job in a clothing store in Washington turned up, so he took it. "I must have been a great manager," says Steve, "the store closed in four months!" He was soon back in music, finding jobs in Washington, eventually being the rhythm section (no bass, no drums) for the Tommy Gwaltney Trio, with Tommy playing clarinet and vibes and then-youngster John Eaton on piano. The trio expanded later, adding bass and drums. Keter Betts, a superb player who has worked with Ella Fitzgerald for over twenty years as Ella's "first call" bass player, was with the Gwaltney group for several years.

One reader of this book in manuscript form noted Steve's "uncynical, open-minded, unenvious outlook." And that's the way he is. He is certainly not quick to put other musicians down. And I have heard Steve praise all kinds of guitar players, from amplified guitar soloists who can butcher a rhythm section to country players like Roy Clark and Chet Atkins. Another manuscript reader noticed Steve's "disinclination to gossip." That's right, too. Unlike too many writers of show biz memoirs, Steve does not gossip and you will find no lewd stories involving musicians, living or dead, in this book. He is too much of a gentleman to do that.

Readers may also notice that a good many of Steve's bandstand colleagues are dead. To list only some of them, by year of death: Irving Fazola (1949), Ray Wetzel (1951), Walter Page (1957), Oscar Pettiford (1960), Israel Crosby (1962), Glen Gray (1963), Nick Travis (1964), Teddy Napoleon (1964), Conrad Gozzo (1964), Hank D'Amico (1965), Boyd Raeburn (1966), Edmond Hall (1967), Red Allen (1967), Willie Smith (1967), Boots Mussulli (1967), Ziggy Elman (1968), Cutty Cutshall (1968), Pee Wee Russell (1969), Coleman Hawkins (1969), Morey Feld (1970), Lou McGarity (1971), Charlie Shavers (1971),

Jimmy Rushing (1972), Gene Krupa (1973), Eddie Safranski (1974), Bobby Hackett (1976), Hymie Schertzer (1977), Joe Venuti (1978), Vernon Brown (1979), Stan Kenton (1979), Mary Lou Williams (1981), Vido Musso (1982), Bernie Glow (1982), Dick Mains (1983), Kai Winding (1983), Vic Dickenson (1984), Trummy Young (1984), Claude Hopkins (1984), Shelly Manne (1984), Jo Jones (1985), Zoot Sims (1985), Benny Morton (1985), George Duvivier (1986), Teddy Wilson (1986), Benny Goodman (1986), Felix Giobbe (1986), Maxine Sullivan (1987), Al Cohn (1988), Billy Butterfield (1988), Mousey Alexander (1988), Roy Eldridge (1989), Will Bradley (1989), Wild Bill Davison (1989), Georgie Auld (1990), Lee Castle (1990), Jimmy McPartland (1991), Bud Freeman (1991), Richard Maltby (1991), and Buck Clayton (1991).

Some of the greatest jazz players ever are among those listed above. And the sad thing is that so many are irreplaceable. Unique is the proper word for many of them, notably Pee Wee Russell, Joe Venuti, Ed Hall, Bobby Hackett, Vic Dickenson, Teddy Wilson, and Benny Goodman. Each was one of a kind. To the knowing ear, their solos were almost always unmistakable, beyond imitation. Though several of these great original musicians had talented emulators (yes, Peanuts Hucko plays something like Benny, as does Bob Wilber), there was no mistaking the real thing.

Veterans of the swing era become fewer all the time. Fats Waller, Chu Berry, Bunny Berigan, Art Tatum, Big Sid Catlett, Jack Teagarden, Johnny Hodges, Cootie Williams, Stuff Smith, Ben Webster, Lester Young, and so many other jazz heroes of my youth, are long gone. Thank God we still have their recordings. Billie Holiday, whose voice was a jazz horn only she could play, died in 1959, as did Lester Young. The first great jazz soloist and unquestionably the most influential of all jazz musicians during the 1920s and 1930s, Louis Armstrong, died in 1971. The most honored bandleader and composer, Duke Ellington, whose swing era band of the early 1940s is generally considered the greatest of all his bands, died in 1974. Earl Hines, the great pianist, died in 1983. Count Basie, whose swing era band was the swingingest big band I ever heard with the greatest rhythm section and most exciting group of soloists, died in 1984.

But some survivors of the swing era, such as Steve Jordan, are still on the bandstand and still able to show anyone with ears how it's done.

That Steve became a "name band" musician in 1939, rather than another year, wasn't only because of his age, twenty, or his musical ability. Because of the popularity of swing music, many new bands, hoping to become "name bands," were created in 1939. Throughout that year, four booking agencies— Music Corporation of America, Consolidated Radio Artists, General Amusement Corporation, and the William Morris Agency—kept adding more bands to their rosters. And most of these bands were led by musicians who had gained prominence as soloists in other swing bands. Square baton-wavers were out, hip jazz musicians were in!

Indeed, in 1939 the dance band business was bigger business than it had ever been before. Officials of the major booking agencies estimated that Americans paid a record-setting $100 million to listen and dance to bands that year. And many sidemen, suddenly known nationally to a large new group of young record collectors and swing band enthusiasts, understandably wanted a bigger piece of the big band pie. They were eager to do what other crack sidemen like Benny Goodman and Artie Shaw had done and make some real money fronting swing bands.

Potential "name" bands created in 1939 were those headed by Harry James, Jack Teagarden, Jack Jenney, Teddy Wilson, Tony Pastor, Bobby Byrne, Johnny "Scat" Davis, Bob Zurke, Teddy Powell, Van Alexander, Georgie Auld, Bob Chester, Coleman Hawkins, Benny Carter, Nick Pisani, Jimmy Mundy, and Wilbur Schwichtenberg (who became Will Bradley). Some of these bands were successful, some were not. Some were successful artistically but not commercially.

And in 1939, competition for the swing fan's dollar was tough: Benny Goodman (by 1937, "The King of Swing," one of the most famous musicians in American history), Artie Shaw (though Shaw disbanded his band in November, 1939, while at the very top, vying with Goodman for popularity honors), Tommy Dorsey, Jimmy Dorsey, Glenn Miller, Woody Herman, Larry Clinton, Charlie Barnet, Duke Ellington, Jimmie Lunceford, Gene Krupa, Jan Savitt, Les Brown, Bob Crosby, Count Basie, Earl Hines, Red Norvo, and Glen Gray. Bands that were decidedly not swing bands such as those led by Hal Kemp, Kay Kyser, Guy Lombardo, Sammy Kaye, Wayne King, Horace Heidt, Jan Garber, Orrin Tucker, Freddy Martin, Eddy Duchin, and Shep Fields (bands jazz people called "Mickey Mouse" or "sissy" bands) provided competition too. As did local bands and territory bands, those that worked in only one city or one area of the country.

Fortunately for the young Steve Jordan, the Will Bradley band was one of the new 1939 bands to survive. Indeed the Bradley band not only made it, but made it big.

Now, after more than fifty years as a jazz professional, it's amazing how Steve Jordan has managed to hang in there somehow during the last few decades, playing his kind of music even though jazz lost the kids (black and white) many years ago to rock, soul, whatever, even though jazz recording became increasingly rare, even though ballrooms became a thing of the past, even though many jazz clubs closed all over the country.

And this is particularly remarkable in Steve's case because he is a rhythm man, not a "star" electric guitar soloist. Big bands left the scene, the jazz audience diminished, but Steve kept on, and keeps on, playing his way on his acoustic instrument. There is no major market for his great rhythm guitar playing, as former Louis Armstrong drummer Barrett Deems said. But as Steve, ever the quick wit, remarked recently, "I couldn't be a rock guitarist because my hair is too short." Steve has worn a crewcut since he joined the Navy during World War II.

I hope this book will introduce some fascinating jazz musicians (many of their recordings are still available) to younger readers. And, for older ones, stir some memories of those now distant days when jazz was—of all things!—popular music. For all generations, Steve and I hope this book might inspire some smiles and a few laughs.

Steve is unpretentious, as is his book, one that surely should not be confused with those somewhat academic studies that present jazz as some kind of problem to be solved, curiously forgetting that jazz, no matter how heartfelt, no matter how artistic, is mainly fun.

I want to thank Frank Driggs, jazz historian and producer of many marvelous LP reissue albums of 78 rpm recordings, for most of the rare photos in this book. Thanks also to photo contributors Dan Morgenstern at Rutgers University's Institute of Jazz Studies and the late Will Bradley. I am also grateful to jazz record collector Sonny McGown for his expert help with troublesome discography details.

1

THE SWING ERA

With Will Bradley and Ray McKinley

My first contact with show business as a kid was Jimmy Durante. I used to mow his lawn, in Flushing on Long Island. He wasn't rich. He had a nice home but nothing fancy. Durante had been big in vaudeville but he didn't work much in the early 1930s when I knew him. A nice generous guy, Durante. He'd give me a half dollar for the lawn job when half dollars were hard to come by.

By age sixteen, in 1935, I liked to clown around strumming a ukulele and making like Pinky Tomlin singing *The Object of My Affection*. Four years later I was a professional guitar player, on the road with the Will Bradley band playing *Beat Me, Daddy, Eight to the Bar*, watching jitterbugs shag and lindy to that thing called swing, rooming with championship character Freddie Slack, and discovering that jazz musicians say and do the damndest things and are more skillful with quick one-liners than most stand-up comics.

There was no big decision on my part to become a jazz musician at age sixteen. But music had always been an important part of my life, and when the swing music craze hit with Benny Goodman, I was ready to swing with it. But you can be sure that I did not envision myself as a member of Benny's band, or as someone who would be playing guitar with many of the finest musicians of his generation.

I grew up near Hell's Kitchen on the West Side of New York, where everyone was either Irish or Italian. I'm both. My mother was an O'Neill, Mae Elizabeth O'Neill, and my father was Dr. Philip Giordano, an ear, nose, and throat specialist known as "the mayor of 44th Street." When he died at age eighty-seven in December, 1977, he was still treating patients in the same office, at 433 West 44th Street, he had when I was a kid. In fact, his patients in 1977 included great-great-grandchildren of some of his first patients. It was, and still remains now, that kind of neighborhood. Many families there have never left, and you'd be surprised at the number of people living there who not only have never seen any other city except New York but have never been on the East Side. It's as if they know their neighborhood and that's all they want to know.

I certainly didn't starve during the Depression, thank God, because my father was a physician. But he had a wife, a mother, and six kids to support. And I remember he once came home with a bushel of potatoes after taking out some kid's tonsils because the father, a grocery store owner, had no cash. Dad even made enough to belong to a country club. No golf, but a clubhouse with a tennis court, handball court, and swimming pool. The Depression did not hit me the way it hit so many others.

My father was eighteen months old when he came to this country from Sicily. My grandfather was a barber when barbers seemed to have all the money. Grandpa believed in the work ethic if any man ever did, and he saved enough to get my father through college and medical school.

Dad wanted to be an electrician because electricity was coming in strong when he was a kid, but Grandpa told him he'd be a professional man or he'd get no help from him and could look forward to working with a pick and shovel. So Dad went to pre-med and med school at NYU. In the summer he sold men's clothing. Work and save, work and save. Maybe we could use more of that in our country now. I know that at nightclubs where I've worked recently it's hard to find help. No one wants to be a busboy.

I grew up with music because music was to our household what television seems to be in most households today: our primary form of entertainment. Only we didn't stare, bug-eyed, at a TV tube. We created our own enter-tainment, as was customary in most Italian and Irish homes in my part of New York. Mother played the piano and Dad played mandolin, guitar, and saxophone. Mother's birthday was always a big musical event because, to celebrate the occasion, Dad would hire a band of five or six players. He'd usually join in on the sax, sometimes leading the band through its stock arrangements in our living room. For us kids, it was much more exciting that television could have been.

Since my father's name was Giordano, the reader may wonder why I'm Jordan. I sometimes wonder, too. One thing is certain: I didn't change my name legally or any other way. It was changed for me, and it all had something to do with nuns. We always talked a lot of Italian in the house, and when my sister Marie and I were going to Holy Cross Academy on 42d Street near 9th Avenue, nuns kept calling my mother, an O'Neill, to say that her children were having a hard time in school because when they talked they moved incessantly from English to Italian and no one at the school could understand them. The nuns suggested we speak more English in the home and may have been the ones to suggest that our names be changed to Jordan in school, to Americanize us more. It all happened when I was around six years old, and I have never had the whole story straight. But since grade school I have been Steve Jordan.

Jazz first came into my life in a major way in 1934, by radio. Most all of the music on radio at that time was what we later called schmaltz, corn, or Mickey Mouse stuff. Guy Lombardo and His Royal Canadians, Art Kassel and His Kassels in the Air, Jan Garber who was billed as "The Idol of the Air Lanes," Rudy Vallee and His Connecticut Yankees, Emery Deutsch, and all the rest. The night that opened my eyes and ears was the night when Ted Fio Rito's orchestra had just finished playing from California and the announcer said something like, "And now we switch you to Benny Goodman in New York for something different." It was different, all right, and I was hooked. I had never heard anything like Goodman's music in my life. Others may have known of the Fletcher Henderson band and some of the other fine black bands that inspired Goodman, but I didn't.

I soon discovered Jimmie Lunceford, too, and in 1937, because of two tonsillectomies, I discovered Count Basie. It happened this way: Two boys had to have their tonsils out, but their father had no money. My father said the tonsils must be removed anyway and they could worry about the money later. Dad even paid the overnight hospital charges. After the tonsillectomies, the father, who owned a radio store with fancy radio-phonograph combinations that no one had enough money to buy, offered Dad one of his best phonographs and a stack of records to pay for the operations. And as brother Ed and I looked over the stack of new records earned by Dad in this trade for tonsils, he found a blue-labeled, thirty-five-cent Decca and asked me, "Who's this Count Bassy?"

I didn't know who "Bassy" was either, but we soon learned. That Basie record—it was *One O'Clock Jump* or *Jumpin' at the Woodside* or *Out the Window*, one of those early Basie swingers—was a revelation.

By this time I had taken some guitar lessons from an Italian teacher in our neighborhood (we were living on Long Island by then) and was playing stock arrangements in high school bands. The teacher was Bartolo Logiudice, my father's uncle and father of tenor saxophone player Don Lodice, a soloist in the Tommy Dorsey band. Two years later I was with a decent professional band led by trumpet player and arranger Vic Hunter and playing fairly well. Hunter had some good players, including alto saxophonist Bill Shine, drummer Lou Fromme, and several others who made the big time later. The problem with this fifteen-piece band was simple enough: we couldn't get enough work. So it became mainly a rehearsal band. And one day a rehearsal with Hunter led to my job with Will Bradley, the first of many "big name" bands I was to work with.

This rehearsal was in the Goldbetter Studios, a kind of schlock joint in the Roseland building near Times Square. All members of our band chipped in—half a buck, whatever—to pay for the studio. And that day in 1939 the Artie Shaw band—making it big with *Begin the Beguine* and drawing the kind of crowds and attention only the Goodman band received—was rehearsing in the next studio. Shaw probably used the studio, schlock or not, because he knew it had a good piano. Shaw was careful about things like that, as I was to learn when I worked in his band a few years later.

During a chat with some of Shaw's players that day someone said that the next big band to hit it big would be the band Will Bradley was rehearsing. I was told that Willard Alexander, the booking agent who had had much to do with Goodman's opportunity for success, organized and was pushing the Bradley band. I was also told that two of Jimmy Dorsey's best players, drummer Ray McKinley and pianist Freddie Slack, had left Dorsey to join Bradley. (Alexander, incidentally, did not have his own office then. At that time he was still with the William Morris Agency.) No guitarist had been hired by Bradley yet, they said, so I figured, what the hell, I ought to try out even though I had no real hope of being selected.

I called the Morris Agency about an audition and was told to call Ray McKinley. Apparently McKinley was to be a kind of coleader. (The band was finally billed as Will Bradley and his Orchestra featuring Ray McKinley, and it was known in the trade as the Bradley-McKinley band.) McKinley told me to come to his room at the Piccadilly Hotel on 45th Street before the audition. I did and, at his request, played some guitar as he was getting dressed. He asked me who I liked on guitar and I told him Allan Reuss and George Van Eps. That seemed to please him. He liked them, too. He said a lot of good players would like to be in the new band, but they couldn't afford most of them. I told him I didn't want to undercut anybody's salary although I hadn't had much experience. He said, understandably, "Well, you have to be good enough." I wondered if I was.

At the audition, I discovered that nine guitarists had already auditioned, including Dan Perri, an accomplished player from Canada who later played rhythm guitar on the Lucky Strike Hit Parade while Tony Mottola did all the melodic amplified stuff, and still later on the Perry Como show. And that day there were three more guitarists ahead of me. I thought they all played well and I became somewhat nervous about playing.

But I got the job. I think they figured I was young (twenty), lived at home, and didn't need as much money as the other guitarists who auditioned. The pay was $125 a week, clear, nothing taken out. Most members of the band were getting more, some around $200 which wasn't bad then since even the most famous sidemen in the business—say, Gene Krupa with Benny— got only about $250, maybe $300 tops. (Although Lionel Hampton says that he joined Benny Goodman for $550 a week in 1936 and that Gene's salary was doubled because of his trio and quartet work in addition to band drumming. Maybe so, but Hamp's figure certainly surprises me. I do know that Cootie Williams, Ellington's great trumpet player, joined Benny in 1940 for $230 a week, which was considerably more than he made with Ellington.) Remember, in those days musicians were paid more than singers. Frank Sinatra made $75 a week with Harry James and not much more than that with Tommy Dorsey.

So there I was, suddenly in the big band business. While more affluent or more brilliant kids my age were off to college, I was off to see America in a band bus. And damned pleased to be making $125 a week. I had no way of knowing that I'd soon be rooming with a nut like Freddie Slack. No way of knowing, either, that I'd still be playing jazz in 1991.

After I came aboard as the band's guitar player, we rehearsed for a few days before opening at the Famous Door on West 52d Street, where the Basie band first set the New York jazz crowd on its ear. This was when that block of 52d Street between Fifth and Sixth Avenues was known as "Swing Alley" or, to musicians, simply as "The Street." When a guy lugging a musical instrument told a cab driver to take him to "The Street," few cab drivers needed further direction. This was where Stuff Smith and Billie Holiday swung at the Onyx, where the incomparable Art Tatum left all other piano players in awe at the Three Deuces, where Fats Waller, Earl Hines, Red Allen, and dozens of other great players jammed at Jimmy Ryan's. This was where—during the late 1930s and early 1940s—you could hear more honest jazz in a single block than could be found anywhere else in the world.

Only small jazz groups worked The Street until 1938 when Willard Alexander and John Hammond got the owners of The Famous Door, Al Felshin and Jerry Brooks, to book Count Basie's thirteen-piece big band. The Basie band was a sensation and The Famous Door began to bring in other big bands. None of the bands that played there made much money—the club could seat only about sixty people—but the publicity and the exposure a band received at the Door, including three radio remotes a week, could be the start of something big. It certainly was for Basie. And in 1939, the Charlie Barnet and Woody Herman bands got a real publicity push at The Famous Door, as did our new Bradley-McKinley band.

On our last day of rehearsal before our Monday opening night at the Door, McKinley told us that Jimmy Valentine, from the University of Texas, who was joining the band as singer, could not arrive until Thursday. We had three airshots scheduled from The Famous Door that week as well as a record session at Columbia. I assumed we would be doing without a singer, but somehow McKinley had heard I could sing a little and he told me to learn the lyrics to the ballads we had been rehearsing because I was going to fill in for Valentine.

"Me?" I asked. "Sure," said Ray, "I can sing but I can't sing ballads. I've got a voice just like a frog."

"So have I," I said.

But McKinley was not convinced and I had to do it. And when our first radio performance came up and I saw that big mike with CBS on it, I could hardly open my mouth. I managed to struggle through the vocals somehow and from our first recording session later that week two sides were produced with Steve Jordan vocals: *The Wind and the Rain in Your Hair* and an American version of *O Sole Mio*. I still have the records and, as for the singing, I can assure you that no one who heard those recordings ever thought that the new Bradley band had come up with another Perry Como or another Dick Haymes. I was glad to see Jimmy Valentine arrive from Texas.

My father came to hear the band at The Famous Door, and soon tenor saxophonist Nick Ciazza, who replaced Peanuts Hucko, and bass player Felix Giobbe, proud Italians, let me have it. They talked Italian to my father, asked me what I knew in Italian—I didn't know much—and told me I was some kind of walking crime. "Your name is Giordano and you call yourself Jordan? And look at the way you're dressed. You look like an Englishman! Okay, your name is Jordan, we'll remember that!" I was twenty years old and not certain whether they were kidding or not. But we became friends. And of all the characters I've worked with in music, Giobbe—a big, bearlike, picture-book Italian with a banana nose, a booming voice, and booming mannerisms to match—was certainly one of the most delightful.

At The Famous Door, once the downstairs of a Victorian brownstone townhouse and only about sixteen or eighteen feet wide, there was hardly room for a big band, and Giobbe and his bass were right next to the kitchen door. The club had a Chinese cook at that time and the continual smell of chow mein and similar fare began to disturb Giobbe's large, Italian nose. In the middle of one tune, he yelled loudly over his shoulder toward the kitchen: "Hey, you can take that mongoose off now! I think he's done!"

One time Felix was high on marijuana. He had smoked only a few puffs but he couldn't take it. We were playing on the Astor Hotel roof and Felix was giggling during a slow ballad. He leaned over to me and said, "Hey man, I played the same line four times!"

Lots of laughs, Giobbe. His father was Luigi Giobbe, bassist with the Pittsburgh Symphony. At age fifteen, Felix won an art scholarship from the Carnegie Foundation and his father decided Felix should study both art and music in Italy. I remember Felix telling me about his days in Italy: "It's wonderful over there. I went around laughing all day long because everybody looked like me!"

Felix returned to study at Carnegie Tech and Duquesne University, then started to play jazz at Nick's, a club in Greenwich Village made famous by Eddie Condon and his colleagues. By the time he was twenty-one, Felix was a member of the Pittsburgh Symphony and also touring with Paul Whiteman. He was later first bassist with ABC. And if you ever visit the Prudential Savings Bank at 390 Avenue of Americas, notice the bank's huge mural—sixty-seven feet by six feet, showing lower Manhattan and Greenwich Village in the early 1800s—done by my old jazz buddy, Felix Giobbe. That job took him eight months. He did a number of other murals including one for an apse commissioned by a church in Italy, and one for the Banco Brasilio in São Paulo, Brazil. First-class jazz player, first-class symphony musician, artist, and memorable clown. That's Giobbe.

And Giobbe's bass sound was as large as his nose. I'll never forget when he broke a bass string while we were playing at a theater in Cleveland. He had to stop playing entirely, because when one bass string goes, tension on the neck of the instrument forces the remaining three strings out of tune. He had to go offstage to fix his bass, and when he stopped playing it sounded like the rest of us—thirteen in number—were out there all alone.

It was when I was first working with Will Bradley, at The Famous Door, that Allan Reuss straightened out my guitar playing in only nine lessons. In those days, Reuss was the best rhythm guitarist in the business. At eighteen he replaced George Van Eps in the Benny Goodman band in 1935, shortly before that band made it big. He was recommended to Goodman by Allan's teacher, Van Eps, and his sound, as well as his rhythmic wallop, helped to give Benny's first great band a special character, a certain distinction. The brassy "killer dillers," sparked by Gene Krupa's drumming and the trumpet playing of Harry James, may have grabbed the general public the most, but that Goodman band's lovely middle sounds, meaning the reed section led by Hymie Schertzer and the rhythm guitar of Reuss, turned many of us on just as much.

By 1939, Allan had left Goodman and was giving teaching a whirl. To do this, he rented a studio, actually one of the little cubicles on the top floor of the New York Band Instrument Company, which was also the Gibson guitar agency in Manhattan. I had gone there as a teenager when my father bought me my first Gibson L-5. Eddie Bell was the New York City Gibson agent in those days, and he repaired guitars in addition to selling them.

The Famous Door on 52d Street was just around the corner from Eddie's Gibson shop, and I was chatting with Eddie about a minor guitar problem one day when he told me that Allan Reuss was teaching upstairs. "No kidding," I said, and went upstairs to meet him. And I was surprised when Reuss said, "Hey, I've heard you, you're playing with Ray McKinley!" I soon arranged to drop in every week for a lesson while working at The Famous Door.

Reuss used no guitar book of any kind. He told me he never used a book, even for a beginner, only a pencil and a yellow pad. He'd sketch out chord diagrams, explain this or that about harmony, and watch what you were doing right or wrong on the guitar fingerboard.

I learned from Allan not to use the first string (the high E) and he emphasized not to use a bar (a flattened forefinger over all six strings, functioning like a capo, is the most common bar [sometimes spelled barre]), which I never used anyhow, but to use the tops of your fingers and in this way get open voicing. Some chord positions he taught were new to me, and considerable homework resulted, as did a tighter, crisper sound. My playing improved after just my first lesson with Allan.

So, I had only nine lessons with him because the Bradley-McKinley band soon left The Famous Door for road engagements, but I will always be grateful to Allan Reuss for teaching me what rhythm guitar is all about. Grateful, also, to the great George Van Eps, who taught Reuss. I suspect Freddie Green was similarly grateful to Reuss and, indirectly, Van Eps. Freddie also studied with Reuss.

While the Bradley band was at The Famous Door, Don Raye came in with the song *Beat Me Daddy, Eight to the Bar*. As those who are old enough should remember, it became a big hit. Once that record came out (and in those days it took about two months from the time of the recording date to the time the records were issued) our band was nationally famous. We were told by Columbia Records that, after only one month on the market, *Beat Me, Daddy* had sold more than 100,000 copies, which is something like a million-seller record now, I guess.

Freddie Slack had been a straight jazz piano player all his life but had to learn the boogie bass in order to play this novelty piece by Raye and Hughie Prince. And Freddie really worked at it. On *Beat Me, Daddy* and other later boogie pieces we did, Freddie played straight eighths, not dotted eighths and sixteenths as some do who think they are playing boogie woogie. And unlike the brass on Tommy Dorsey's *Boogie Woogie*, our brass section played straight eighths, too, as did Joe Wiedman, our jazz trumpet soloist. Wiedman, from Chicago, was a wonderful player who never received the recognition he deserved, being a much better trumpet player than many who ranked above him in *Down Beat* and *Metronome* popularity polls.

Slack may not have been as accomplished a boogie player as Bob Zurke with the Bob Crosby band, but he was certainly good at it. The thing was that after *Beat Me, Daddy* and other similar pieces our band played, Slack became stuck with eight-to-the-bar. He told me playing boogie "was fun, for a while, but now I've got to play it all night long." Freddie became bored with it, but the public demanded he play it and Freddie liked attention and applause.

Our recording featuring McKinley singing about a piano player in "the little honkytonky village in Texas who plays better by far when they yell beat me, daddy, eight to the bar" put our band on the map. And other recordings kept us there, notably *Scrub Me Mama, With a Boogie Beat* (based on *The Irish Washerwoman*), *Rock-a-Bye the Boogie, Scramble Two*, a flag-waving arrangement of *Hallelujah!*, *All That Meat and No Potatoes* and *Celery Stalks at Midnight*. As for that last one, someone explained the curious title to me this way: Celery was a drummer who would get high and then go strolling—or stalking—down the highway at midnight. But I never heard of a drummer named Celery, so that explanation may or may not be true.

With these record hits to draw good crowds wherever we played, the band made it. We all got raises from time to time and started to make good money.

When the band began, Will Bradley lived in Rego Park (right next to Forest Hills) in a nice rowhouse. Within a year and a half, he had a beautiful apartment on Park Avenue.

Bradley, a fine, meticulous trombone player who did not tolerate sloppy playing, was once told by a player during rehearsal that he had a "wrong note" on his manuscript. Will told him, tongue in cheek, "There is no such thing as a wrong note. It's a *misplaced* note. The note's all right, it's just in the wrong place, that's all. Put it where it belongs."

We had many fine players in that band. Peanuts Hucko was in the original band, plaing tenor, not clarinet. Les Robinson, later with Goodman and Shaw, played lead alto for a while and he had a most beautiful, singing vibrato. First trumpet player Bunny Snyder, a big jolly guy who smoked cigars, was able to command a brass section with the quality of a Jimmy Maxwell in my opinion. After World War II, Bunny was in Broadway show bands and became an executive at Local 802 in New York.

And there was trumpet player Pete Candoli from Mishawaka, Indiana. Best known for his later work with Woody Herman and Stan Kenton, Pete was only eighteen years old when he joined us, and he had played with Sonny Dunham's band when he was seventeen. Pete could play. He was also quite a wit. We were carrying bags into the hotel on the road one day and Pete said, brightly, "Nice looking hotel. How much are the rats?" Tony Faso added: "You don't have to worry about your suitcases, gentlemen, a roach comes out and carries it for you. It happened the last time I was here." Formerly married to singer Betty Hutton, Pete later married singer Edie Adams. I heard him with Edie in Washington more than thirty years after he had played with Bradley and his trumpet was as powerful as ever. His younger brother, Secondo, known as Conte, is also a fine trumpet player. I wonder who taught them how in Mishawaka, Indiana.

Bass player Doc Goldberg, who replaced Giobbe when Felix decided to stay in New York, was another lively character in that Bradley band. I arrived in Penn Station one day for a train trip with the band in a new kind of corduroy jacket I'd picked up at Roger Kent's clothing store. It had a wide wale instead of the usual pinwale. And Doc's first words to me were, "Who wrote the lyrics to that jacket?"

Practice is the name of the game in music and one of the trombone players in this band—Bill Corti, an Italian from Chicago—told me a story about practice I've never forgotten. His father was his trombone teacher and one day he angrily told Bill, "I didn't hear you practice today." Bill explained that he had a pimple on his lip and pointed it out to his father. "That pimple's no excuse," said his father. "What you do is take your trombone and put your mouthpiece right on the pimple and you go POW! and break the pimple! And then you PRACTICE!"

Bradley and McKinley often argued with one another and Freddie Slack argued with both of them. The arguments usually concerned tempos. Bradley, who really ran the band, usually won those squabbles, leaving McKinley grumbling with remarks like, "Okay, Bismarck, have it your way!" Despite McKinley's "Bismarck" talk, I think the blond, slender Bradley was of Scandinavian descent. He certainly looked more Danish than German. His name was changed from Wilbur Schwichtenberg to Will Bradley because bookers insisted that the public wouldn't get a name like Schwichtenberg straight, and that Wilbur Schwichtenberg and His Orchestra wouldn't fit on a marquee. Arthur Arshawsky probably changed his name for a similar reason, becoming Artie Shaw.

I made fifty-two sides (78 rpm recordings) with the Bradley-McKinley band but wasn't on the band's first recording date. This was made just after its first engagement, at the new Kenmore Hotel in Albany, before the band returned to New York for further rehearsal and a job at The Famous Door. Bill Barford, one of the band's arrangers, played guitar in Albany and on that first recording session. He later decided to stay in New York and write arrangements rather than go on the road, thus the open guitar chair, which became mine.

Our first road trip was certainly memorable for me. This came right after The Famous Door job and consisted of a week at the Totem Pole Ballroom in Norembega Park, in Newton, near Boston. Band members who had cars stayed in Boston, and the rest of us stayed in boarding houses near Norembega Park. I used to get up early in the morning, rent a canoe and paddle up the Charles River, which was filled with lily pads, all the way to Waltham and back. I found it beautiful up there, so marvelously different from New York.

In October, 1939, Sy Oliver, the trumpet player and fine arranger for Jimmie Lunceford, left Lunceford because he wanted to go to college. But Tommy Dorsey talked Oliver into postponing his college plans to write for the Dorsey band. He succeeded by offering Oliver much more money than he had made with Lunceford. When the first Oliver arrangements for Dorsey were heard, it was plain that this was a completely different Dorsey band. Some of the Bradley players thought it was wrong for Tommy to go that route, sounding a good deal like Lunceford, but without the Lunceford band's loose feel and reed section timbre. Oliver gave the Dorsey band a Lunceford touch but his arrangements for Dorsey were characterized by screaming brass. Dorsey newcomer Ziggy Elman (from the Goodman band) led the trumpet troops, and another remarkable soloist, drummer Buddy Rich, thundered the heavy artillery, in marked contrast to drummer Davey Tough's softer approach while with Dorsey. (Tough played louder later with Woody Herman.) With Oliver pieces such as *Well, Git It,* the Tommy Dorsey band was no longer primarily a "pretty" band, which disturbed some, but it was surely a more exciting band. And when Will Bradley heard the new Oliver-Dorsey sound, he said, "We ought to get something going like that."

Will knew I had worked with arranger Vic Hunter and that Vic liked the Lunceford style, so he asked me if Vic might want to try some Oliver-type music for our band. But by that time Vic had quit music and was working at a dry cleaning shop somewhere in Brooklyn, I didn't know where. I couldn't locate him, but I did know Billy Moore, a trumpet player with Lunceford, and I knew that Billy was writing a good many of Lunceford's charts. I contacted Billy, and soon he was writing many arrangements for our band in his spare time while still working for Lunceford. *All That Meat and No Potatoes,* which sounds like a Fats Waller line, was one of the most popular pieces Billy did for our band.

For those too young to remember the big band era, "name" bands then played stage shows in movie theaters in addition to working in nightclubs, hotels, and ballrooms. And for one week in New York the Bradley-McKinley band did the improbable: We worked the Paramount Theater and the roof garden of the Hotel Astor at the same time. We were booked into the Paramount for four weeks with comedian Danny Kaye, who was making his first major engagement after the show *Lady in the Dark.* The next two weeks we were signed to work the Astor roof. When we were held over two weeks at the Paramount, we (1) played three daytime shows at the Paramount, (2) played the dinner dance at the Astor for an hour, (3) returned to the Paramount for the fourth show, (4) went back to the hotel for an hour and a half, (5) returned to the theater for the fifth show, (6) and then back once again to the Astor to play until 1:30 A.M. We did this for a full week but had to cancel out of the Paramount for that other week. The trumpet players simply couldn't take it. Lips are not designed for that much tooting. Ask any trumpet player.

Recording was much different in those days than it is now. For one thing, every recording had to be under three minutes. I think what we aimed for was 2:50. We had to shorten our arrangements frequently to fit them on a 78 rpm record. After one record session, we went directly to a theater date, and on the way there Will said that when we get to such and such a number we should "play the cuts."

It was the wrong thing to say. Halfway into the tune on stage, all we had was cacophonous noise. Half the band thought he meant *observe* the cuts, the other half thought he meant forget the cuts and play the whole arrangement. It was like a train wreck! Perhaps he should have said play *through* the cuts. McKinley ended it all with crashing cymbals and a loud drum roll. It was the kind of thing an audience seldom sees. The crowd laughed along with us, Will explained what had happened, and we took it from the top again, this time playing through all the cuts. I remember hearing about a similar thing happening to a tap-dancing comedian. He had to make some cuts in his music for his act and handed out red pencils to members of the band. They made the cuts properly, but when the show began they discovered that the theater spotlights were red and no one could see the cuts.

One time at the Circle Theater in Indianapolis we could hardly play our opening theme, *Strange Cargo*. To understand why, you have to know that bandleader Ray Noble—who came to the United States from England in 1934 and fronted a band including Bud Freeman, Charlie Spivak, Glenn Miller, Claude Thornhill, Johnny Mince, and Will Bradley (and is also well remembered for writing *Cherokee* and *Goodnight, Sweetheart*)—was known in the music profession as the most meticulous, fussiest, and sharpest dresser in the business. The clothes he wore could not be purchased off the rack, if you favor understatement. Well, on this afternoon as the newsreel was ending and the curtain on stage was going up, with Will about to give the downbeat for *Strange Cargo*, he said: "Play good, fellows, Ray Noble's tailor is in the audience." We all broke up and it was the strangest, partly played *Strange Cargo* the Bradley-McKinley band ever struggled through. The audience must have thought we were all drunk or high on marijuana or something.

And I'll never forget a theater engagement with Anita Louise, the movie star. Not because of her act but because of something Freddie Slack said two weeks later. Anita was different from most movie stars we occasionally shared the stage with because about all most of them could do was smile. Anita could actually play the harp. And she wasn't bad at it, but Freddie Slack didn't like her because she was on the cornball side when she tried to play jazz and because, at one point in her act, she would say, "Now let's all get lowdown and boogie woogie!" Slack said that kind of talk was corny, beneath contempt, and insulting to musicians. Two months later we were on the road, working in a ballroom in Maine. Behind the ballroom was a band room that had only one john. After a set one night, a few of us went to the men's room and found that one john in use. Freddie had to go, and he yelled: "Now let's all get lowdown and piss in the sink!"

Although Slack was unquestionably the band's number one character, saxophonist Nick Ciazza could also do the unexpected. One time in Asheville, North Carolina, Freddie and some of the other players were going to a jam session somewhere after the job. Nick and I had other plans, Lord only knows what, I forget. I borrowed roommate Slack's car and Nick said, "Let me drive because I haven't driven in a long time." So I turned the wheel over to Nick. He was going only about forty in a thirty-mile speed limit zone when a cop stopped us and asked to see Nick's license. Nick told the cop he didn't have one, adding, "I used to have one but that was a long time ago." Then with the words "will this do?" he handed the cop his musician's union card. I drove the rest of the way that night.

Playing with the Bradley-McKinley band was exciting for a twenty-one-year-old jazz-happy young man like me. My girl was the band's lovely nineteen-year-old brunette singer, Lynn Gardner, a *Down Beat* cover girl, my favorite and only girl. We talked about marriage at one time but the war came, I went into the Navy, we went our separate ways, and she married Al Durante, Jimmy Durante's nephew. With Bradley I was making $175 a week with few expenses, and the band was a good one with quite a following of cheering kids wherever we played.

Alas, jazz lost the kids years ago and I doubt if we will ever again see the kind of enthusiasm for jazz music that we had during the late 1930s and early 1940s, the swing era.

You've got to remember, too, that back then a kid could take his girl dancing to Glenn Miller at Glen Island Casino for five bucks. That was more than enough. Today a kid would have to ask his father for at least $25 for the same kind of evening. And of course few kids today have been exposed to the wonderful sounds of a good big band. There are few ballrooms anywhere now, only clubs, and most of these have rock groups or records by rock groups, either of which is injurious to the ears.

Jazz musicians, not rock singers, were heroes to many kids then. Most *Down Beat* subscribers were fans, not musicians. And they could tell you all about their heroes known as Louis, Benny, Fats, Big Tea, Chu, Cootie, Pres, Rabbit, Lips, Bunny, Stuff, Big Sid, Buck, Sweets, Chick, Zutty, Rex, Fatha, the Hawk, and Tricky Sam. And they knew who the incomparable Art Tatum was, in marked contrast to a piano player I worked with forty years later who had never even heard one Tatum recording and didn't seem to want to hear one but was trying to play something similar to jazz on the piano. It's a different world of music now.

And kids in the 1950s did not invent words like *hip* or *groovy.* We used all that lingo in the 1930s. And we didn't say *hep,* we said *hip.* Ray McKinley, in fact, was beyond *groovy.* He said once, after the band had finished a real swinger, "Man, that was *right down the crease*" rather than *in the groove.*

Freddie Slack left the band in 1941 to start his own band. Ray McKinley left to do the same thing. Shelly Manne, only eighteen, replaced Ray. I stayed, as did singers Lynn Gardner and Terry Allen. Will wanted to keep Mahlon Clark, a very good young clarinet player, but Mahlon had promised Ray he'd go with him, and subsequently received considerable attention for his work with McKinley.

Pearl Harbor all but killed the big band business. By 1942, musicians were being drafted left and right. As Will is quoted in George Simon's 1967 book *The Big Bands:* "We were playing in Detroit when they took six men from us all at one time—most of them trumpets. From there we had to go directly to Denver. Now, where could you find six men in Denver to replace the guys we'd lost? I had no idea, so I didn't even try. I just gave up the band."

I wasn't present for the end of Will's band, having left months before to accept an offer from Artie Shaw. I was with the Shaw band four months, until it disbanded in February, 1942, when Artie went into the Navy. I was soon in the Navy, too. When Will Bradley called it quits with the band he was twenty-nine or thirty, married, and with two kids so he didn't have to go to war. He went back to the studios in New York, where he had worked before under such conductors as Andre Kostelanetz, Victor Young, and Raymond Paige before getting into the big band business.

In 1943, while on leave from the Navy, I phoned him and his wife, Pat, answered. She said Will had left for a radio show but that he'd love to see me and I should come right over. She had tickets for his radio broadcast with Kostelanetz, so I went and heard some gorgeous sounds. A trombone piece was featured. The trombonists were Will, Buddy Morrow, and Billy Pritchard. It was great legitimate playing. Beautiful! I had a beer with Will, we talked about the old band, and it was a pleasant reunion. Nice guy, and superior trombonist, Will Bradley. The best of all trombonists, Glenn Miller used to say, which is a fine compliment indeed coming from such a selfish stiff as Glenn Miller. Will died in 1989 at seventy-eight.

McKinley is more or less retired, but I assume he is still involved with music somehow. I heard him guest star with an Air Force band not long ago and he still sounded fine on drums. After Maj. Glenn Miller's mysterious disappearance in December, 1944, on a flight from England to France, Tech. Sgt. McKinley took over Miller's Air Force band that included Peanuts Hucko, Mel Powell, Carmen Mastren, and other prominent jazz players, and from 1955 to 1966 he led a "Glenn Miller" orchestra that was certainly commercially successful. Helen Miller, Glenn's widow, owned the Miller arrangements and Tex Beneke took over the "Miller" band when Ray decided he didn't like the salary offered.

In 1977, the Bandstand record company, in California, reissued dozens of recordings of the Bradley-McKinley band on four LPs. The company kindly sent copies to me. I don't even know how Bandstand got my address. Unlike some reissue sets that boom up the bass and jack up the brass, the sound is true to the original 78 rpm recordings. To some ears, these records may sound dated, but they still sound good to me. The Bradley-McKinley band was one of the better bands of the swing era and I was happy to be a part of it when I was a young man about one and twenty discovering the joys of life and big band jazz.

Freddie Slack and Buttercup, Who Became a Lion

His wife, Jean Ruth, said, "He's not like anybody else. I love him, but I can't stand to live with him." Singer Bob Eberle, who worked with him in the Jimmy Dorsey band, said he wasn't a Section Eight but a Section Nine. And I understood what they meant about my close friend Freddie Slack.

Freddie was not just different. He was one of a kind. He said and did the damndest things. He even had a pet lion he called Buttercup.

Freddie would blow his stack immediately if anything bothered him. I almost went to jail with him in Pensacola when I was with his band in 1946. He didn't like the ham and eggs in a restaurant, and he threw the plate of food up against the wall. The police came and arrested him. I tried to restrain him but he socked one of the cops. Another cop tried to twist his arm, and he somehow sprained that cop's back. As he was holding onto the door of a patrol car preparing to swing at still another cop, the cop hit him on the left hand with a club. Freddie yelled, "If anything further happens to me tonight it's going to be nationally known in the morning!"

They took him to jail, and the rest of the band got on the band bus because we had to travel to New Orleans for our next engagement. The band manager stayed with him, and Freddie was released from jail the next day. He rejoined the band with bandages on his head and left hand. His boogie playing wasn't much good that night.

Freddie got drunk and got upset easily, but he was pleasant and very funny most of the time and I loved the guy. I knew him better than anyone else in the Bradley band because I was his roommate on the road.

He discovered the bow and arrow while we were with Bradley. A movie short featuring archer Howard Hill, a big guy with a black mustache who went shark hunting with bow and arrow and shot a sixty-five pound bow, turned him on, and a book by Hill entitled *The Witchery of Archery* inspired him. He studied this book all the time on our band bus. He bought a sixty-five pound bow that you had to pull all the way back with your right arm to make it function. I could only get it about halfway back, but stocky Freddie, who was stronger than he looked, could pull it all the way back.

When we were playing in a ballroom in Illinois somewhere—I forget where, when you are on the road with a band it's easy to forget just where you were even the month before—Freddie found a nearby deserted handball court. He bought some balloons and tacks, then tacked the strings holding the balloons all over the wall. After much practice, he could hit those balloons pretty well.

Later he bought hunting points made of steel. He said animals don't have a chance after a rifle telescope sight but did against a bow and arrow because an arrow is not as accurate as a bullet. He was all for giving animals a better chance.

One night in 1940 we were driving in his '39 Mercury and as we went around a curve we could see two little beady eyes shining in our headlights. "That's a deer!" yelled Freddie.

He stopped the car and rushed to the trunk to get his bow and arrow. As he was starting to load his bow, he looked at me and said, "I can't do it." We could hear the deer run away. "How the hell can I kill something as beautiful as that? I'm just going to do target shooting from now on. I thought I could go deer hunting but I can't."

It reminded me of what had happened to Kerm Black, a childhood friend. His father had told him: "If you can kill an animal you've got to eat it. Target shooting is one thing, but if you kill a bird you are going to have to eat it." And after my friend killed a robin with a BB gun, his father *did* cook it and *did* make him eat it. "You kill only for food, not for sport or trophies," the father insisted. I agreed with the father and with Freddie about his reluctance to shoot a deer.

In 1942 when I was in the Navy in Norfolk, Virginia, I got a letter from

Freddie telling me he was drafted into the Navy but, he said, "I don't think I'll stay there." And he didn't. He was in the Navy only ten days. As he later wrote to me, "I was in over the holidays, playing the organ in church, and playing the piano for the kids on Christmas."

This happened at the Farragut Training Base in Idaho. And Buttercup, his pet lion cub, played a major role in the short Naval career of Freddie Slack.

Buttercup came into Freddie's life shortly before he entered the Navy, while he was on the road with his band in southern California. As both Freddie and his roommate, saxophone player and arranger Les Baxter, told it to me, Freddie was driving around for no special reason and stopped at an animal farm. There he was much taken with a lion cub. He bought the cub, that weighed about thirty-five pounds, and put it in the bathroom of the hotel room he was sharing with Baxter.

Les came in later, went to the bathroom, and came running out. "Freddie, there's a lion in our bathroom!" he yelled.

"But he's only a baby," said Freddie.

Freddie kept the baby and—as babies will—it got bigger and bigger. He became too big to handle on the road, so Freddie brought him to his home in Beverly Hills and wife Jean Ruth, who was the overseas disc jockey Beverly in the radio show "Reveille with Beverly" that inspired a movie of the same name.

In about one year a lion develops its full frame but is skinny. And incredible though it may sound, after one year Buttercup weighed 300 pounds and was still growing. Freddie had a bulldog collar made for Buttercup and used to walk him on a leash. He told me that one time as they were going around a corner, a man with a police dog on a leash was coming around the corner the other way. The police dog recoiled as they came face to face and let out a loud yelp. Buttercup ran like hell, dragging Freddie along, and hid behind a tree. Freddie tried to explain to Buttercup that lions eat dogs but Buttercup didn't seem to understand. Buttercup had never seen a dog before and feared the unknown.

On Freddie's first day in the Navy, he got his uniform, hat, shoes, sheets, and—although he considered it beneath his dignity—stenciled his name as required on every article. He then went through the prescribed routine of packing and unpacking his duffle bags, because the chief told him he had to practice folding all day long. As anyone who has been in the Navy knows, if you can survive the first day, you're okay.

As the lights were about to be turned out at 9 P.M.—make that 2100—the chief came in and said, "Leave the lights on, everybody up!"

He then told all the boots to open their duffle bags.

"Are you serious?" Freddie asked.

The chief was serious.

"Well," says Freddie, "I've packed and unpacked this duffle bag twenty times today and I'm not going to do it again."

The chief told Freddie that he would indeed do it and also informed him that someone in the barracks had lost a Parker 51 fountain pen and it might have been stolen.

"Who was it?" Freddie said. "What do those pens cost? Fifteen dollars? I'll give him the fifteen dollars right now but I'm not going to open that bag again."

"Can you afford to pay for everything that everybody might steal from all men in the barracks?"

"Yes, I can," said Freddie, "and I intend to. But I'm not going to open that bag."

I asked Freddie what happened next.

"I opened the damned bags, what else? The guy said if I didn't I'd be taken to the guardhouse immediately."

Two days later, Freddie was scrubbing the floor somewhere and a second-class petty officer came in and said, "Slack, the lieutenant wants to see you right away!"

Freddie strolled up to the lieutenant and said, casually, "What's up?" Everyone on the base knew who he was, a big star. (That year his band produced Capitol Records first million seller, *Cow-Cow Boogie,* with vocal by Ella Mae Morse.) The lieutenant told him "a big crate was just delivered here with a lion in it and it was addressed to you, Apprentice Seaman Frederick Slack."

"Buttercup is here!" said Freddie, joyously.

By then Buttercup weighed 420 pounds.

The lieutenant told Slack that "we have to get it out of here, and I just want to know from you where you want it sent."

"If Buttercup goes, I go," Freddie replied.

"Well, you're going anyhow," the lieutenant said. "The lion's going this afternoon. It will take a couple of days to get you processed out of here."

So Freddie gave the lieutenant Martha Raye's home address. "Send the lion to this address," he said.

A few days later he was out of the Navy. On the day of his discharge he met a sailor, back from combat, also being discharged. "I've got plenty of money," Freddie told him. "Let's go to Seattle. I know a great jazz club there." So they went to Seattle by train, got drunk together, and late that night Freddie called Martha Raye from a hotel in Seattle to see whether Buttercup had been delivered.

Martha, then married to Nick Condos, who with Steve Condos made up the terrific tap-dancing Condos Brothers act, said, as Freddie recalled: "Yes, you damn fool, the lion's been here for three days. The dogs won't come in the house, the lion's in a crate in the basement, we don't know what to feed it, and it *roars!* The neighbors are complaining."

"Just go down and pat him," Freddie told Martha.

A few days later Freddie got the lion from Martha and brought it back, somehow, to his home in Beverly Hills. Freddie and Jean Ruth were later told by police to get the lion into the zoo and not to ever walk it on the street. The lion, well over 400 pounds and getting bigger all the time, would curl up on Freddie's bed like a pussycat.

Freddie finally decided he had no choice and would have to take Buttercup to the zoo, so he called the curator and explained he was donating an African lion in good shape, one with all his required shots.

As both Freddie and Jean Ruth told the story to me, the two of them and Les Baxter were walking the lion up a hill to the curator's office at the zoo, passing some Brahma bulls from India when one of the bulls uttered a big, deep moo. Buttercup bolted and ran, hiding behind a tree as he had done when confronted by the police dog.

Buttercup didn't know that lions eat bulls. He had never seen an animal that big before. Nor heard such a deep moo.

After settling Buttercup down, to make the trip up the hill easier, Freddie, Jean Ruth, and Les managed to get a large wheelbarrow and somehow got Buttercup into it, then began to cart Buttercup up the hill again. Jean Ruth held her hands over Buttercup's eyes so he wouldn't see the Brahma bulls. Luckily, none of the bulls mooed this time.

With the leash on his spiked bulldog collar, Freddie walked Buttercup into the curator's office. The curator immediately jumped on his desk.

"What's the matter?" asked Freddie. Buttercup was sitting down, looking kind of stupid, waiting to be told what to do next.

The curator was frantically pushing buttons, and soon two men came in with long sticks with wire loops on the end. They started to poke at Buttercup, hooking the loops onto his collar.

"Don't do that," Freddie yelled. "Where's the cage? I'll put him in the cage." The uniformed keepers looked scared to death, Freddie said.

With Freddie handling him gently, Buttercup went into a cage and the necessary papers were signed.

A month later, when Freddie and Les were back on the road with Freddie's band, the band had an engagement near the zoo. "Let's go out and see how Buttercup's making out," Freddie suggested.

They discovered there were three other lions in the cage with Buttercup. It was quiet at the zoo that day but Freddie was embarrassed as he became aware of people staring at him, incredulously, as he leaned over the guard rail saying, "Here, Buttercup! Here, Buttercup!" Freddie said he couldn't tell Buttercup from the other lions but hoped that Buttercup would remember him. He tried to get Buttercup to come over to him for nearly an hour. But Buttercup never came. He apparently didn't remember Freddie at all. Buttercup had become a lion.

You never knew what Freddie would get involved with next. By the time he had his own band he had forgotten about his fascination for the bow and arrow and was into darts. He'd throw them in the hotel room at anything. He'd make a target on the wall and shoot. One night he was lying in bed with a bag of darts and was throwing them at the ceiling.

"Freddie, you can't go to sleep with those darts up there, one could get loose and come down on your head, point first," I said.

"Don't be silly," he said, and rolled over and went to sleep. I got up and got his darts out of the ceiling.

I'm told that when Freddie was with Jimmy Dorsey, Jimmy had to pay for an old piano because of Freddie. The band arrived for a gig at a country club in Valdosta, Georgia, and found a beat-up piano that was way out of tune, almost unplayable. Freddie took the front off the piano so he could hear it better and then pulled out some of the hammers. As the evening went on and Freddie's frustration with the instrument mounted, he yanked out more and more hammers. The club discovered what was left of its piano the next morning, wrote to MCA, the agency handling the Jimmy Dorsey band, and a month or so later MCA took the price of the piano out of Jimmy's take. Jimmy Dorsey, one of the nicest guys in the music business, didn't get upset, I'm told. "Well, it was a miserable piano," he told Freddie.

Freddie loved pipes. Expensive pipes. He had quite a collection. And cashmere sportcoats. And Burberry topcoats. He had a full-fashioned raglan one with red, white, and blue houndstooth checks, and another mustard one with heather in it. He loved to look classy. He was that way as a sideman in the Bradley-McKinley band when he was making only $175 a week, the same salary he earned with Jimmy Dorsey.

Joe Glaser, his booking agent, would break up the Freddie Slack band now and then because of Freddie's drinking. Drinking cost Freddie money, and it cost Glaser money, too. When I was with Freddie's band, one time Glaser told Jean Ruth to tell me—since I was Freddie's best friend—that if we were at a theater or anyplace else and Freddie sent me to a liquor store to get him some gin or Scotch, and he found out about it, that I would never work in the music business the rest of my life. Well, I was about twenty-five years old, had never bought Freddie any booze and certainly was not about to buy him any and end my career in music. Could Glaser, booker for many big names including Louis Armstrong, have done such a thing? I didn't want to find out.

I remember a theater show we were doing with Peter Lorre in Cleveland. Lorre did an act called "The Man With the Glass Head." (Don Rickles later picked this up and used it, with Lorre's permission, in nightclubs long before Rickles became nationally known.) It was a fascinating portrait of a man going mad. Lorre had a valet with him when he met Slack backstage and quickly told his valet, "Get the Scotch." The valet brought in a case of Scotch. I don't know how much of that case Freddie polished off between shows but when he came out on stage he fell down and couldn't play. That's why Glaser used to break up his band.

Strange things were always happening to Freddie Slack, or so it seemed. One time we had to take the ferry across the Chesapeake Bay to Virginia Beach (there was no tunnel then) and on the ferry floor, right beneath the door lock of Freddie's car, there was a hole about as big as a quarter where you could see the water. And as he locked the car door he dropped the key and it went through that small hole into the Chesapeake Bay.

"Well," said Freddie, "I'll have to get another key." He acted as it if were nothing to worry about, and since it was an hour-and-a-half ride, he went to the top deck and wasted $20 worth of arrows shooting at and missing seagulls.

The car had to be towed off the ferry, with the brakes on.

You never knew what was going to happen next with Freddie Slack.

In 1948 he was living in the San Fernando Valley, and he had a beautiful Siamese cat, a cat of legal size, not a Buttercup. One morning he found his cat dead in a wooded area behind his house. Half the cat was gone. Freddie was horrified.

"Then," he told me, "I became furious because I figured a coyote had come down from the mountains and gotten him. I bought a whole pile of dog food, spread it all over the ground and sat on the back steps all night with a .22 rifle waiting for the bastard."

No coyote showed up. I told him that I'd heard coyotes can smell humans and won't come close when one's around.

"Well, maybe I should've put another cat out there and waited inside at a window," he said.

Freddie was found dead in his Hollywood apartment in 1965. Due to natural causes, they said. He was fifty-four years old. I suspect those "natural causes" involved alcohol.

For all his faults, I loved the guy. He was quite a piano player, too.

Underrated, Forgotten Bands

There are sounds that are not musical sounds that I miss today. I miss the sound of a wooden frame screen door slamming. I miss the sound of a milkman's horse softly clop-clopping in the wee hours. I miss the sound of a hand lawnmower clicking as you wake up in the morning. And I certainly miss the sound of a steam locomotive in the distance going *wooooooo*. That's a great sound. I also miss the sound of airplane piston engines and the sound of loose tire chains sloshing in the distance on a quiet snowy night. Today's generation rarely hears these sounds.

Another sound seldom heard, at least in a big city, is warmly remembered. Years ago, on a dark, dreary, cold November day I was walking up Seventh Avenue toward Central Park. It was a typical New York City scene, with taxi drivers yelling at bus drivers, bus drivers blowing horns to get cars moving, a guy chopping up part of the roadway for the gas company, and a traffic officer blowing his whistle. Suddenly there was a loud honking from above. Everything seemed to stop cold and I looked up, as did everyone else in the area. The honking was from wild geese. There must have been a hundred of them flying in perfect **V** formation. They had come from northern forty below Canada to nest in the Carolinas. Nature! Flying over a metropolis! As I stared at this beautiful, almost incredible phenomenon in the grey sky, I experienced an emotional feeling, almost sadness, and I could only think "now, *that's the truth*." Those wild geese didn't realize that they had interrupted civilization for a few seconds. They didn't have pneumatic drills or jobs or armies or defense plants or chaos, as we civilized beings did. That was the only time I've ever seen and heard such a glorious display. It didn't cost anything and I'll never forget it.

As for musical sounds, I miss the sounds of good big bands. Yes, despite Count Basie's death, the Basie band is still on the road at this writing. But there are only a few other big bands worth hearing. Some of the big bands today, including Maynard Ferguson's, as well as the band of young men once led by the late Woody Herman (who managed to keep his band going until his illness in 1987), are involved with incorporating contemporary popular music, which means rock or something akin to rock, into the big band sound. It is usually not a happy involvement, and in any event it is not the sound I hear in my mind's ear when I remember the big band days. Big bands did not have to scream, brassily, for attention then.

Say "big band era" to me and I think of places as well as music. Including some beautiful scenes. In 1939, before I joined the Bradley-McKinley band, I remember what it was like when Glenn Miller played at the Glen Island Casino near Fort Slocum in New Rochelle, New York. The casino was on Long Island Sound, and there were always small sailboats anchored in the cove around the club to hear Miller's music in the moonlight. Youngsters on these boats lay back, listened, and hugged and kissed as the music wafted over the water. It was a lovely place, a lovely time, and I keep thinking nothing quite like it will ever happen again. I understand why the kids who listened to Glenn Miller's music from Glen Island Casino for free in their small sailboats and rowboats have a hard time understanding their children who pay high prices to hear ear-splitting electronic noise at a crowded rock concert.

I remember, too, enjoying the smell of salt water between sets in the ballroom at the end of Atlantic City's Steel Pier and at the other waterfront piers up and down the East Coast. The salt air might not have been good for pianos, but it was good for the psyches of big band musicians.

I also remember some good bands that jazz critics have forgotten, if they ever even knew about them.

When I was seventeen, I was impressed with the band Charlie Randall had working in Armonk, New York. A few years later I heard he was in South Carolina. I have no idea what became of him. With luck, and proper booking, perhaps he would have had a "name" band. One hit record might have put this band on the map. *Woodchopper's Ball* certainly helped Woody Herman. *Cherokee* did much to make Charlie Barnet famous. *Beat Me, Daddy* did the same for the Bradley-McKinley band, as mentioned earlier. And *Begin the Beguine*, a song and an arrangement Artie Shaw never cared much for— it was the B side of his best-selling Bluebird record—surely helped to make Shaw popular almost overnight. But in Artie's case, if it hadn't been *Begin the Beguine,* it would have been some other tune. (The A side of this famous record, trivia fans, was *Indian Love Call* with vocal by tenor sax player Tony Pastor.)

Buddy Rogers, the movie star famous to many because he married Mary Pickford, had a good band, too. Gene Krupa came to the Goodman band from the Rogers band, which originated on the West Coast and worked in the Midwest. I wondered at the time why it never came to New York, and years later discovered the reason: Willard Alexander, then with the William Morris Agency, handled the bookings for the Rogers band as well as the new Goodman band. Benny was starting to make it big at the time and Alexander didn't want the competition of the Rogers band working in the same area as the Goodman band. Rogers was no standout musician himself although he played several instruments, mainly trombone and trumpet, but his band's version of *Bugle Call Rag* was fast and overwhelming. I think the band might have made it in New York's Pennsylvania Hotel, for example, if it had been given the chance. The band did get some air shots out of midwestern hotels late at night, but the band never caught on no matter how hard it tried. Again, perhaps a hit record would have made this band successful.

One of the best bands I ever heard, and certainly one of the best bands of 1936 and 1937, was the Hudson-DeLange orchestra. I'll never forget the way it did *Looky, Looky, Looky, Here Comes Cookie* when I first heard the band in Rye Beach, New York, at the Rye Beach Casino on the roof of Alice Foote MacDougald's restaurant. The band had taste and class and it could swing!

Eddie DeLange was a big Irishman, about six foot three with red hair and freckles. That night he was wearing a cream-colored gabardine suit, no shirt or tie, but a moss green velvet ascot. He had rust-colored suede shoes to match his rust-colored mustache and a baton about three feet long. He sang with a deep, whiskey-toned baritone and carefully accented all s's. His way of singing *You Go to My Head* was distinctive, to say the least.

Will Hudson seldom traveled with the band. He stayed in New York and just kept mailing arrangements to the band wherever it was. Hudson was a prolific arranger, having written for McKinney's Cotton Pickers, Cab Calloway, Jimmie Lunceford (*White Heat* and *Jazznocracy* were two Hudson pieces Lunceford made famous), Don Redman, Fletcher Henderson, Benny Goodman, and many others. Hudson also turned out stock arrangements by the score.

DeLange, a Penn graduate with a Phi Beta Kappa key, fronted the band with verve. He was a big juicer, I was told, and he always seemed to be having a ball. I remember one night when he stepped off a foot-high bandstand, tapped a boy on the shoulder, and danced a delighted young girl around the ballroom with style and grace, winding up to applause from the other dancers. Quite a showman, Eddie DeLange. In current vernacular he would be called "something else."

The band's tall, skinny guitar player, Guy Smith, played excellent rhythm and could play solos like Carmen Mastren. I remember he favored Epiphone guitars, as Mastren did. He was one of the best in the business at that time and I have no idea what happened to him. After the war I never heard of him working in the studios or anyplace else. Gus Bivona was in the Hudson-DeLange band, too. And one of its singers was Fredda Gibson, who became a radio and recording star as Georgia Gibbs. Hudson and DeLange collaborated on many songs, Hudson writing the music and DeLange the lyrics. Their best known tune is undoubtedly *Moonglow*, written in 1934. Older readers may also remember some of Hudson's instrumentals such as *Organ Grinder's Swing*, and the band's theme song, *Sophisticated Swing*.

Hudson and DeLange split in 1938. Hudson kept the original band while DeLange organized a new band. Neither band did well. Will continued to write for big bands, including Glenn Miller's Army Air Force band. DeLange wound up writing for the movies and did some lyrics for one of the great composers of popular music, Jimmy Van Heusen. Remember *Deep in a Dream (of You)*? "My cigarette burns me, I wake with a start. . . ." He died in 1949.

Sonny Burke, a big, good-looking guy who had led a college band at Duke University, had a group made up mainly of Boston musicians. It played well. I heard the band in rehearsal in 1939 and bought the few Okeh records it made. Burke, an arranger, styled the band to sound something like Jimmie Lunceford's. Burke later led a band of Detroit musicians originally fronted by tenor saxophone player Sam Donahue. Sonny became the leader when Donahue left to join Gene Krupa. When Donahue left Krupa in 1940 he wanted his band back, and the players decided they'd do better with Donahue, by then nationally known, fronting the band. Burke then became an arranger for Charlie Spivak and Jimmy Dorsey. He was also a fighter pilot during World War II, proving that not all musicians in uniform spent their time in service playing music. (Bandleader Larry Clinton was also an Air Corps pilot.) Burke went on to become one of the most prominent arrangers and conductors in the West Coast recording studios, producing many albums for Frank Sinatra and other famous folk.

Bob Allen, who had sung with Hal Kemp, had a wild, swinging band that also played some beautiful dance arrangements. But the band never made it commercially. Allen was a handsome, movie-star-looking, heart-throb type with a deep, rich voice. He became a leader after Hal Kemp died, but his band was never to be confused with the "sweet" band Kemp led. When most all the big bands were breaking up because of the war, Allen was able to keep going because he and some of his key players were not drafted.

One reason the Allen band was exciting was the remarkable trumpet playing of Randy Brooks. Listen to an old recording of *Young Man With a Horn* under his own name. I never heard anybody play a trumpet like Randy Brooks. *Anybody.* He had sound, guts, power, range. When I first heard him while on ten-day leave from the Navy, I couldn't believe my ears. I had no idea that the Allen band was so good when I went to hear it at the old Pennsylvania Hotel in New York. Indeed, the only reason I happened to hear the band was because Lynn Gardner was singing with the band. As mentioned earlier, Lynn and I had developed a close friendship during our days with Will Bradley. When I was with Saxie Dowell's band in the Navy, Saxie kept telling me how great Randy Brooks was. I was doubtful. I never heard of a Hal Kemp musician getting up and playing a jazz solo. Kemp didn't have that kind of band. I kept thinking, what does Saxie know? Then I heard Randy Brooks. Saxie knew. Randy Brooks was unbelievable.

Brooks married blonde bandleader Ina Ray Hutton. Many men of my generation will remember Ina Ray for the eye-catching way she wiggled in tight gowns while leading her band with a long baton. Billed as "The Blonde Bombshell of Rhythm," they said she made six gown changes on every gig. Not a musician, she had been in the Ziegfeld Follies of 1934 when Irving Mills picked her to lead an all-girl band in 1935.

Brooks, from Maine, formed his own band in 1945, and teenager Stan Getz was one of his sax players. Randy's band came too late. The big band era was ending and the band didn't last long. He and Ina moved to California. A stroke ended Randy's trumpet playing and he died in a fire in 1967.

Teddy Powell and Bob Chester had underrated bands, too, but more about those bands later.

Moving forward past the swing era, the band that Les and Larry Elgart had in the 1950s was a wonderful band, I thought. This was the band with no piano and the rhythm guitar up front. The guitar player used a micro-phone, no amp, and on the road the guitarist was Turk Van Lake, who went on the Russian tour with Benny Goodman in 1962. In the recording studio, the guitarist was usually Barry Galbraith. I couldn't understand that and told

Les Elgart my view of the matter in Charlie's Tavern one time. "Good lord, I can see why you figure the kids you use on the road are not as polished as studio men here, but you ought to use Turk on the recordings. He'd like to do the record dates." Les said, "Well, you know Barry." I told him, "Yes, I know Barry, have known him longer than I've known Turk, but Turk can do exactly what Barry can do for you on the recordings. He does it with you on the road." Les only replied, "Well, you know we hire a contractor for the records." Well, Dick Maltby used a contractor, too, but he instructed the contractor to call me and Dick Perry and Kenny Arzburger for the record sessions.

Barry Galbraith is an accomplished rhythm player who sounds a good deal like Freddie Green, but Turk can play almost identically to Freddie Green and that is the sound they wanted. I thought Turk should have been on those Elgart recordings and still think so. The last I heard of Turk he was living on Staten Island and not doing much of anything. There is no crying need for good rhythm guitar players now.

Larry Elgart came into Freddie Slack's band when I was working for Slack after the war. He played lead alto and he was a little stiff. Johnny Wade (real name Wojdag) was on baritone sax and he played impeccably, something like Ernie Caceres. I had worked with Larry Elgart and with Wade before in the Vic Hunter rehearsal band when Bill Shine or Julie Schwartz played lead alto and Larry played third alto.

After Larry had been with the Slack band for a week or so, I was talking one day to Wade on stage just before our show, with the movie still on and the curtain closed, when Larry came over and told Wade that he was playing lead alto and didn't like the way Wade was trying to push him into phrasing differently, and that if he couldn't hear what he was doing then he, Larry, could. He said Freddie Slack was going to hear about it. Wade told him to go fuck himself and Larry just turned and walked off the stage. Soon thereafter Larry quit the band on the pretense of another job and Johnny Wade became the lead alto player. Wade sounded like Bill Shine playing lead and it was a different Slack sax section. It really swung. Wade, a delightful guy, is living in the Washington, D.C., area now, buying musical instruments for a suburban high school system. Still plays, too.

Larry and Les Elgart were quite different. Larry was the one who saved all the money he was making, while Les had to borrow money all the time. Les always seemed to have a woman on his arm and thought nothing of buying diamond bracelets for his girl of the moment. Les could really play but when the Elgart band broke up he had nothing. Larry, who had doubled as road manager, was a quiet type who saved his bread.

With Artie Shaw and Teddy Powell

I joined Artie Shaw as the Bradley band was about to call it quits, in 1941, and I was with Shaw until he broke up his band to join the Navy in 1942. I had no problems with Shaw. He was always nice enough to me. He liked jam sessions backstage and he'd often get me involved, saying, "Get the guitar, Steve, let's play a few tunes."

Shaw had a good ear. He once stopped a band rehearsal because he said my G string was a little flat (it was). Unlike many leaders, Shaw knew the guitar string setup (E-A-D-G-B-E). You can always hear the D string, but Artie heard the G string, the weakest string, too.

When I was with him, this oft-married man was wed to Betty Kern, Jerome Kern's lovely daughter. Artie told me that Kern had a habit of writing letters to bandleaders, whether he knew them or not, after he heard them play one of his songs on the radio. He'd compliment them or—when he didn't like the arrangement—tell them that his song shouldn't be played that way. Shaw said he was most familiar with such Kern criticism long before he married Kern's daughter. (His other wives included Lana Turner, Ava Gardner, Kathleen Winsor, Doris Dowling, and Evelyn Keyes, all famous actresses save for Winsor, famous for her best-selling novel *Forever Amber.*)

I'm told that Artie hasn't played his clarinet for many years, even for fun. That's too bad. After all, he was some clarinet player with a gorgeous sound in all registers, especially the upper register. And he sounded like no one but himself, as is typical of the great ones.

When I was working with Shaw at the Capitol Theater in Washington in January, 1942, Les Brown's band was at a nearby club, the Casino Royal, which is long gone (the fancy Capitol Theater is gone, too.) One night between shows, Artie, trumpet player Spots Esposito, and I went to hear Les's fine band. Artie was soon sitting in. While talking with Les as Artie played with his band, it soon became plain that Les was in awe of Artie. He told me he was sorry he hadn't practiced more as a kid. "I feel like a fool playing clarinet after listening to Artie or Benny. That's why I let Abe play so much." He was talking about Abe Most, a terrific clarinet player.

I remember one night in Chicago when the Bradley-McKinley band wound up the last show at the Chicago Theater at 11 P.M. and a few of us went to hear Les Brown's band at the Blackhawk Restaurant. We left our table and stood in the front of the band as it played *Mexican Hat Dance,* featuring Abe Most. Les Brown is a better clarinet player than he thinks he is, but, as he knows, no match for Abe. Though he was the leader, Les split clarinet solos with Abe because he loved to hear him play. This night as Abe completed three bristling choruses on *Mexican Hat Dance,* smiling and bowing to great applause, Les yelled, jokingly, "Abe, that was wonderful. If you ever do it again, you're fired!"

When Shaw broke up his band to go into the Navy, I knew I'd be going into the service soon, too. But I did work with Teddy Powell's band for two weeks before joining the Navy in March, 1942.

Powell's drummer, Lou Fromme, called and told me Powell needed a guitar player because Guy Smith, whom I remembered for his fine work with the Hudson-DeLange orchestra, was leaving. I joined Powell at the Log Cabin in Armonk, New York.

Powell had an excellent band in 1942 but you won't find much if anything about it in jazz history books. One reason it's not remembered as it should be is the recording ban imposed by musician's union chief James Petrillo on August 1, 1942, that lasted two years (out of this did come a union-controlled fund into which the record companies paid a fee for each record made). Only those who heard the Powell band in person knew anything about it. Well, there were some records but not enough to establish the band in any way. One of these records was *Sans Culottes* featuring Lou Fromme and it was great.

We had a wild trumpet player, Johnny Austin, formerly with Jan Savitt. Two fine tenor players, Ron Perri and Pete Mondello. An accomplished baritone player, Larry Mollinelli, with me in the Bradley-McKinley band. And an excellent piano player, Billy Roland, who later went on NBC staff and stayed there.

And we also had Fazola, whose real name was Irving Prestopnik. When he was a kid in New Orleans, he was the only one in his group who could read music, so he got the name Fazola, not for *do-re-mi* but for *fa-so-la.* Fazola was short but weighed about 300 pounds. He was known for his drinking and his absolutely beautiful clarinet sound, which had made him a famous Bob Crosby Bobcat. Fazola was only thirty-seven when he died in 1949.

Lou Fromme's wonderful drumming gave the Powell band an enormous lift. Fromme played like a white Jo Jones. He really did. Lou was later with Artie Shaw, right after World War II, and Harry James, but I have no idea what happened to him. He's another standout player who is not in the jazz encyclopedias and should be.

Powell wasn't much of a musician, but he was determined to have a top rank band and hired the best players he could find. One good trumpet player we had was Dick Mains, who was only seventeen years old when he joined Powell. He later worked with Ray McKinley and Benny Goodman before joining the Army, where he played with the United States Army Band for twenty-nine years. Dick told me he had played in seven Presidential Inaugural parades. Is that a record? He retired as a master sergeant in 1975. I worked with Dick on a one-nighter in 1978 and his chops were as good as ever. And I remember a question he had for the audience when asked if he played requests: "Well, do you want to hear something new or something *good?*" Mains died in 1983.

Powell was a big-hearted guy and some of his players took advantage of this fact. Felix Giobbe, my bass-playing chum from the Bradley-McKinley band, was with the first Powell band in 1939, a band that went over well at 52d Street's Famous Door. Gus Bivona was the clarinet player then and George Koenig played lead alto. Both players were capable of working with Goodman or anybody else. (Indeed, both later worked with Goodman.) Giobbe told me that every once in a while one of Powell's players would go to Teddy with a telegram. A phony telegram. They'd send telegrams to themselves, reading something like this:

DEAR GUS. WILLIE SCHWARTZ LEAVING. NEED LEAD CLARINET. LIKE YOU TO QUIT WHATEVER YOU'RE DOING AND COME WITH MY BAND AS SOON AS YOU CAN GET TWO WEEK NOTICE. WHATEVER YOU'RE GETTING I CAN GIVE YOU $25 A WEEK MORE. GLENN MILLER.

Or, if not Glenn Miller, a similar message from another big-name band leader.

Then the telegram would be shown to Teddy Powell with an appropriate remark such as, "Gee, Teddy, I have to show you this," and Teddy would give the musician a $25 a week raise if he could, or at least $10 or $15 after almost begging the man not to leave.

According to Giobbe, after Bivona left the band and was replaced by Hank D'Amico, a few weeks later Hank pulled the same stunt. Felix said he did it, too, as did Pete Mondello. Teddy apparently never caught on. The average salary in the Powell band then was $125 to $150 a week, with no taxes taken out, good money for single guys then.

During my two weeks with Powell in Armonk, the band members would pool cars and drive up from New York. Fazola was living over an Italian bakery on 10th Avenue on the West Side. One night in the band room he was eating a sandwich on soft Italian bread, and the pretty brunette singer with the band, Peggy Mann, said, "Gee, that looks good. Can you get me a loaf of that?" Fazola said, "Sure, I'll bring you a loaf tomorrow." And he did. Only the loaf of bread from his bakery friends was in the shape of a penis with testes. He handed the bag of bread to her in front of a few guys and as she opened it she blushed but managed a laugh. Anyway, it was good bread. Fazola had a great, if somewhat strange, sense of humor.

After those two weeks with Powell, and with the draft about to reach me, I told Teddy that if I waited to be drafted I could wind up as an Army cook or something because there were more musicians than dance bands in the service, adding that I had an opportunity to join the Navy and be assigned to a new Navy band that Saxie Dowell was forming in Norfolk. Powell understood. He said the whole band business was going to blow up anyway since everyone was being drafted. He wished me well.

Larry Mollinelli was already on two-week notice and soon Larry and I were on the way to Norfolk to join the Navy. We were "Lee Volunteers" and getting in the band Saxie Dowell was forming was supposed to be guaranteed if we joined in Norfolk. It worked out that way, too. On my next gig, I was playing guitar in a sailor suit.

World War II Years in a Sailor Suit

World War II was the beginning of the end for the big band era. Glenn Miller and Artie Shaw were not the only bandleaders to put on military uniforms. And because so many top musicians were in service, capable sidemen were hard to find. Shaw's Navy band that played in the Pacific Theater included Conrad Gozzo, Johnny Best, Max Kaminsky, Sam Donahue, Dave Tough, and Claude Thornhill. Benny Goodman, 4-F because of sciatica that had required surgery at the Mayo Clinic in 1940 (an operation that did not solve his back problem), gave up his big band because of personnel problems and concentrated on small groups. Only a handful of good big bands remained on the road, notably Duke Ellington, Count Basie (minus Lester Young, Buck Clayton, and Jo Jones who were in the Army), Harry James, and Woody Herman's exciting "First Herd."

As for me, like many name band sidemen, I spent much of my time in the military playing music.

I went into the Navy in March, 1942. Saxie Dowell, who had been featured with Hal Kemp, was the only professional musician at the Norfolk Naval Air Station, and the station didn't rate a band because it didn't have enough men assigned there at that time. But Saxie had been told that he could have a band if he could find the musicians. (Right next to the station was the Norfolk Naval Training Station, which had an eighteen-piece dance band.) So Saxie found some musicians, ones like myself who knew they would be drafted soon anyway. As a "Lee Volunteer" from Norfolk, I was soon at the air station and eventually we had a band.

We were all only seamen first class with no musician rates. And as seamen first class we could play music only in our spare time until the base got bigger, then we were to get musician rates. We spent much of our time scraping gum off the bottoms of theater seats, building ballparks, and cleaning up recreation areas. We rehearsed in the evening or on our days off. We played at the officer's club, for enlisted dances, for picnics in the woods, and on street corners to sell war bonds. We'd mop and swab off the stage before playing, but no one in the band resented doing that because that's the way it was.

We had a prominent big band arranger and saxophone player, Deane Kincaide, and a good trumpet player, Kenny Williams, from Cleveland, who also did some arranging for the band. Other able musicians in the band included Hal Leonard (first trumpet), brothers Eddie Slejko (sax) and Stan Slejko (bass) from Cleveland, Larry Mollinelli (baritone and alto saxes, clarinet, flute) who came with me from Teddy Powell's band, and Harry Terrill, formerly Teretsky (lead alto sax) from the Mitch Ayers band.

Though best known as an arranger, Kincaide is a fine tenor saxophonist who plays something like Bud Freeman. He also doubles trombone, clarinet, and flute. For our band in Norfolk he wrote some marvelous, wild things that featured the entire sax section sounding like Bud Freeman. We had six saxophones in this band (seven when Saxie Dowell played along) and when they stood up for one of Deane's Freemanesque choruses, it was unlike anything I had ever heard, then or now, from a sax section. Imagine a Bud Freeman improvisation, in harmony, scored for six or seven saxes. That's what it sounded like. Too bad none of these "unknown" Kincaide arrangements were ever recorded. Deane replaced Bud Freeman in the 1938 Tommy Dorsey band (when Bud left Dorsey to join Goodman) and he told me he was so nervous about replacing Bud that he almost didn't show up.

Deane was writing for Ben Pollack's band in 1932, did many of the big band Dixieland translations that made the Bob Crosby band famous in the late 1930s, and has also written for Benny Goodman, Woody Herman, Tommy Dorsey, Ray Noble, Ray McKinley, radio and TV network studio bands, and Lord only knows who else.

I don't know how much he studied formally, but he has always written contrapuntal music. Take one of his third saxophone parts and it will be a pretty melody by itself. Counterpoint is in his blood. And, believe me, Deane didn't need a piano to write arrangements. All he needed was pencil and manuscript paper.

Richard Himber discovered this after asking Deane to do an arrangement of a tune Himber liked for his big dance band at the Essex House Hotel in New York on Central Park South. Himber had a good orchestra, no swing band, but no sissy band either, meaning it didn't sound like Sammy Kaye or Blue Barron. A good many fine musicians who were determined to stay home and get away from the woes of traveling with a swing band played with Himber at the Essex House or with George Hall and later Vincent Lopez at the Taft. Dean began to work on this arrangement for Himber at the Waldorf cafeteria one night after he had finished a sax job with another band. Between gulps of coffee, he pulled some manuscript paper out of his pocket and began writing out the bass line for the Himber assignment. Deane always begins with the bass line, adding the harmonies and melody later. He once told me that when you know a song but can't figure out the chords, if you can hear the bass line in your mind you will have all the chords. And he's right.

While Deane was sketching in the bass line at a table next to the cafeteria's front window, tuxedo-clad Himber passed by, noticed Deane, and came in to say hello.

"Hi, Rich," said Deane, "I'm just starting your arrangement."

"You can't be," said Himber, "there's no piano in here."

"I don't need a piano," Deane said, factually.

But Himber insisted he had to have a piano. Deane told me that he finally agreed to go with Himber to his apartment that night where Himber promptly made him sit down at the piano.

"I'm going to bed," Himber told Deane, "and I want to hear that piano!"

Deane proceeded to work on the arrangement at the piano but his fingers never touched the keys.

Some time later Himber got out of bed, charged into the living room, and told Deane: "Dammit, I don't hear any piano! I'm paying for that arrangement and I want to hear the piano!"

"Oh, all right," said Deane. As he finished the arrangement at Himber's apartment early that morning he hit a chord every now and then simply to appease Himber.

Back to the war years. While I was playing Deane Kincaide arrangements at Norfolk, my two younger brothers were fighting the Japanese in the Pacific.

Brother Ed, two years my junior, was a good tenor saxophone player in high school and college. He was also quite a fullback and went to Niagara University on a football scholarship. Ed looks today as he did then—210 pounds, six feet tall, bull neck, cantaloupe shoulders, and not an ounce of fat. He won All-American honors and was to try out for the Pittsburgh Steelers when he graduated in 1943 but he was Navy R.O.T.C., went immediately to Notre Dame for ninety-day wonder school, and became an ensign. Despite his athletic and musical skills, he wasn't involved in either sports or music in the Navy. He was a gunnery officer on a landing craft support (LCS) ship in the Pacific that was involved with intercepting kamikaze suicide planes.

In March, 1945, Ed knew that our younger brother Joe, nineteen, was on Iwo Jima as a combat infantryman with the 5th Marine Division when Ed's ship was beside this small, volcanic island that played such a major role late in the war. A few days after the invasion of Iwo, when there seemed to be less fighting on the beach, Ed jumped off the deck into a passing DUKW and went to the beach to see if he could find Joe.

Ed said that he had walked only about twenty feet when he was tackled from behind by a Marine. The marine explained: "It might seem quiet, sir, but don't stand up around here. Crawl wherever you're going. There are snipers around."

Ed asked where the unit's command post was and the marine pointed it out. At the C.P. he was told that Joe was in a foxhole at a certain point on the perimeter and that he would be able to find him okay because Joe had liberated, from the Japanese, a wind-up phonograph and one record by Jimmie Lunceford that he played constantly. Ed crawled toward the front and soon heard the unmistakable sound of Lunceford's band playing *Belgium Stomp*. They had a great reunion, complete with K-ration lunch, as well as Lunceford. Ed gave Joe his .45, since Marine infantrymen carried only rifles, and Ed knew the automatic would be useful in close fighting. Then Ed returned to his ship. That was the last time anyone saw Joe. While on a scouting mission, he was killed by shrapnel from a grenade. I'll not forget the date, nor will Ed: March 13, 1945.

Joe had been due—with the remnants of the Marine 5th Division—for R and R leave in Honolulu and probably would have survived until the Japanese surrender in August of that year if the Army had been permitted to bring in the 10,000 fresh, combat-ready troops it had waiting off the beach in transports. When Joe was killed, the island was secure except for snipers, but this was the one operation in the Pacific that the Marine Corps ran completely. The Army was not allowed to help on Iwo for four more days, presumably so the Marine Corps could get *all* the credit for the operation. I assume this decision was made by Marine Lt. Gen. Holland Smith, commanding general of the Fleet Marine Force, Pacific, who headed the Iwo Jima Task Force. Perhaps General Alexander Vandegrift, the Marine Corps commandant, and Fleet Admiral Chester Nimitz may have had something to do with the decision, too, I don't know. Perhaps some military historian knows. All I know is that 5,931 Marines were killed and 17,272 were wounded on Iwo Jima, by far the highest casualty total suffered by the Marines in any Pacific operation. Why a tiny handful, like Joe, had to be killed after the island was secure, with the Army waiting to come ashore for mop-up work, is a puzzle that has infuriated me ever since his death.

Well, at least Joe died with the sounds of Trummy Young and Willie Smith still ringing in his head. He was apparently killed shortly after the reunion with Ed. Joe had enlisted in the Marines at age seventeen. I remember how he loved the Marines. He didn't mind sleeping in a tent. He always loved hiking in the woods and the great outdoors. As a kid he would shovel snow from the whole sidewalk on our block in Flushing, in front of seven houses, just for fun. He said he'd like to stay in the Marines the rest of his life. He did. But he never reached the age of twenty.

Ed went from Iwo to Okinawa for eighty days and from there to a Naval hospital for treatment of combat fatigue. Later he did some high school football and baseball coaching and was a podiatrist at Red Hook on the Hudson in upstate New York before retiring and moving to Ocean Pines, Maryland. Still plays tenor sax now and then, too.

The most famous musician lost in the war was Glenn Miller. He left on a flight from England to France in mid-December, 1944, and the plane was never seen again.

I never worked for Miller but I do know he was not popular with his players. Freddie Slack said that when Miller was on his heels, he'd see him and guys in other bands would see him and hand him ten bucks from time to time to help him out. (This was when he was trying to organize his first band. He could have worked but he quit playing. He was too busy to play and he had few dollars and no backing.) But when he became big, he wouldn't even notice these same people when he passed them on the street. He wasn't social and he didn't care.

I know that his Air Force band musicians didn't like him. A number of them made that plain to me. As enlisted men, they were doing menial tasks all the time and they knew it took only a call from Major Miller to put an end to that. But Miller didn't make such calls.

Miller couldn't play nearly as well as his Air Force players—Mel Powell, Carmen Mastren, Peanuts Hucko, Trigger Alpert, Zeke Zarchy, Bernie Privin, Hank Freeman, and Ray McKinley included—but he was the major and he let them sweep the floor, so to speak.

One day I was discussing the curious circumstances surrounding the death of Hitler with one of Miller's prominent Air Force musicians. "Oh, Hitler isn't dead," he said, "and I know where he is. He's down in South America hiding out with Glenn Miller."

He was joking, but the depth of his feeling about Glenn Miller was crystal clear.

Twelve Weeks at the Paramount with Sinatra

When I worked with Frank Sinatra, he wasn't known as Ol' Blue Eyes. He was the incomparable Frankie Boy to his large army of adoring, teenaged girls. This was when I was the guitar player in Raymond Paige's forty-two-piece orchestra that backed Sinatra for twelve weeks at New York's Paramount Theater.

Sinatra could get $10,000 a week at the Waldorf's Starlight Roof then. But the Paramount had signed Sinatra to a five-year contract for about $500 a week when he left Tommy Dorsey in 1943 and held him to it. Though the $500 per week was peanuts to what he could have been making elsewhere, it was big money when compared to the $150 a week, or whatever, he made with Dorsey. He had been thrilled when the Paramount—then managed by Bob Witeman—had first signed him for $500.

To find room for the forty-two-piece orchestra, the Paramount had to move the huge organ to the side of the theater, where Don Baker played it for audience sing-alongs. Violinists, viola players, and cellists occupied the space where the organ had been.

One day during the third or fourth week of the engagement, I drank quite a bit of beer with some of the other musicians between shows. I got back just in time to put on my jacket and bow tie and get on stage. Remember, the stage rises, so you can't sneak off, you have to walk off the stage. I was in the front row, close to Sinatra, and right in the middle of *Brahms Lullaby* I realized I had to get to the bathroom quickly. Too much beer. Unfortunately, too, in the middle of the arrangement, every other player cuts out, with only guitar behind Sinatra as he sings "go to sleep, safely rest . . . " I was holding my stomach and fearful of an embarrassing bladder accident. Noticing my problem, the piano player filled in behind Sinatra as I stood up and walked off the stage. Some people giggled and others probably thought I was sick. Sinatra looked around in surprise. After the show, I went to Frank's dressing room and said I was awfully sorry it happened. He told me not to worry because he understood how such things can happen. But a week later, in a different part of the show, it happened again.

I wondered how I could face the guy. This time, he said, ironically, "It's only the Paramount, I don't care." But he did care even though the money wasn't much. I told him it wouldn't happen again and it didn't. But a week later, around Christmas, a group of kids were in front of the stage with presents for Sinatra's kids, Nancy and Frank Jr. Paige kept putting packages all around the stage and some were lined up beside my music stand. Sinatra came over quickly and told Paige: "Don't put them there, Raymond. The guitar player won't be able to get out!"

I enjoyed my twelve weeks at the Paramount with Sinatra, whom I found to be a fine guy, despite those two emergency bathroom exits. The orchestra, playing Axel Stordahl arrangements, was beautiful, and after the last show at the end of the engagement, we were invited to Toots Shor's banquet room for a great party, food and booze courtesy of Frank Sinatra. Duke Ellington and his wife were among the guests.

I didn't see Sinatra again until 1972 when he came into Blues Alley where I worked in Washington to hear pianist Monty Alexander, whose playing he admired. As he was leaving, I approached him to say hello and mentioned that I had worked with him at the Paramount in 1944. The only thing he said was "Ya know, we had forty-two guys on that stage?" He may or may not have remembered my emergency exits—I did not bring them up—but he did remember that orchestra.

Shortly after the Sinatra job at the Paramount ended, I was back at that theater for six weeks in the Vic Schoen band backing up the famous Andrews Sisters. They were swingers.

Patty, the glibbest and friendliest of the three sisters, talked with me and drummer Irv Kluger about music and nearly everything else all the time. She had never heard Mabel Mercer, the sophisticated British singer who came to the United States in the late 1930s after years at Bricktop's in Paris, and wanted to hear her. She asked Irv and me if we could take her to Eddie Condon's—she knew Condon and Wild Bill Davison, his cornet star—and then maybe to hear Mabel, a singer Frank Sinatra, Lena Horne, and many other top singers admired. She didn't want to go to clubs by herself, she explained.

We were delighted to escort Patty. She loved the jazz at Condon's and we went to a club in the East 50s to hear Mabel Mercer. Mabel seemed thrilled by Patty's presence in the audience and by Patty's great and obviously sincere praise for her singing. And Patty insisted on paying all the tabs and taxi fares.

I never saw her again after those six weeks at the Paramount, but I've always been glad I could add Patty Andrews to my list of favorite people.

With Bob Chester, Unsung Big Band Hero

You won't find him in *The Encyclopedia of Jazz* or *The New Grove Dictionary of Jazz,* but to my mind Bob Chester was one of the unsung heroes of the big band days. His band before the war may have been too much like Glenn Miller's—the same voicings for the reeds with the clarinet on top—but the Chester band I worked with after the war was no Miller carbon copy at all, and it could swing.

The Chester band was the first one I worked with after I came out of the Navy in 1945. I don't remember exactly when I joined the band because I didn't go back to work right after I took off my sailor suit. I didn't have to. I had a lot of Navy back pay and wanted to be with Grandma and Dad at home, not in some band on the road.

When the back pay was getting low, I called guitarist Allan Reuss, the best in the rhythm guitar business, to find out what was going on. He said I had called at the right time because a job with the Bob Chester band would be opening up in two weeks. He had been working with Chester but was set to join the Harry James band on the West Coast. He told me to come to the Park-Central Hotel that night, to introduce myself to Chester and tell him that he had sent me to play. That's what I did, and I had played the first two sets by the time Allan arrived. I got the job right then, although Allan played the rest of the night and the rest of his two-week period.

Chester, an extremely nice guy, didn't have to be a musician to survive. Anything but. He was surely one of the wealthiest bandleaders. Even richer than Charlie Barnet, maybe. Chester's stepfather was head of the Fisher Body Corporation in Detroit. Bob was not a great saxophone player by any means but he was a good one, much better than some thought. And he had many excellent musicians in his 1945 band.

The pianist was Teddy Napoleon, later with Gene Krupa and other big names. The drummer was Irving Kluger, who went on to work with Boyd Raeburn, Stan Kenton, Artie Shaw, Dizzy Gillespie, and many others. Our lead trumpet player, Ralph Muzzillo, one of the best, had been in the Will Bradley band with me and had also been with Benny Goodman and Jimmy Dorsey before the war. Most of the trombone solos went to Leon Cox, who played with great wallop and originality.

Leon was always in a fun mood. On the road in a diner with him one day I ordered a ham sandwich and he ordered hot roast *beast.* Like Napoleon, Cox left Chester to go with Krupa, and he's the one who played that great trombone solo on Krupa's original big band recording of *Lover.* I later worked with Leon in Richard Maltby's orchestra.

I remember, too, that just after I got out of the Navy I let my hair grow a little but then decided to go back to the Navy kind of haircut and have worn it in crewcut fashion ever since. At that time, most musicians had ducktails with lots of hair on the back of the neck. I hadn't seen Leon for some time when he spotted me on the street, noticed my crewcut, and yelled, "Hey, man, great haircut! Think it'll heal?" I have no idea what happened to Leon Cox, a terrific trombone player.

Anyone who saw that Chester band should remember our singer Betty Bradley. She was a stunning brunette, exceptionally well stacked, with black eyes and cream-colored skin. She looked like what movie stars ought to look like and it's a wonder Hollywood didn't sign her up. And could she sing!

I worked with Tommy Dorsey's band for three nights at the same time I was playing in Bob Chester's band. Here's how it happened.

The Chester band was at the Adams Theater in Newark. We finished our last show at ten o'clock. Tommy Dorsey's band featuring Gene Krupa, who had just been released from prison (I'll discuss his marijuana rap later), was working nearby in a huge club underneath the Mosque Theater. This restaurant, one of the largest I've ever seen, was run by Frank and Vince Dailey. Frank had been forced to close his famous Meadowbrook because of gasoline rationing. One night at the Adams Theater, I got a call from someone—Tommy Dorsey's road manager Bullets Durgin, I believe—telling me that the wife of Dorsey's guitar player, Dinny Sandoli, was ill and that Tommy needed someone to fill in for him. He wondered if I could make it by the second set. I said I thought I could and managed to do so by jumping off the stage of the Adams Theater as soon as our show there ended and running the few blocks to the Mosque Theater. Tommy said hello, I noticed Krupa behind the drums, and in a few minutes I was playing with Dorsey.

I did this for three nights until Dinny returned. His wife recovered and he was most grateful for my pinch-hitting. He said he would be getting money that night and he had it all figured out so I would get three days of his pay. I didn't know what he was making but I knew he needed the money because of doctor and hospital bills and I told him I certainly didn't want to take any money for helping him out. He kept insisting but I never took the money. I was making enough with Chester. I was single, and I knew he'd need it.

During the six months I was with him, Bob Chester had a good band, no doubt about it. But we kept losing musicians to other bands—Cox and Napoleon to Krupa, for example—because the Chester band never settled down anywhere. It was on the road all the time. One-night stands continually. Once in a while we'd get a week in a theater but even the theater dates were usually split weeks, say three days in a Toledo theater and three days in another Ohio city theater. Top musicians liked the band and liked to work for Chester. They stayed as long as they could, but kept leaving to get away from the road.

In 1947, when I was with Stan Kenton, we played in a ballroom somewhere that had a two-band policy. When we got there we discovered that the other band was Bob Chester's. I didn't know one guy in this Chester band, proving again the constant turnover he had. They played before we did and I said to one of my Kenton colleagues, "Now, that band is really swinging!" And it was. You'd think the Chester players might be scared to death competing in the same hall with the powerhouse Kenton band, but that was not the case. Those Chester guys just kept cooking all night.

Bob Chester died about ten years ago. I saw nothing about his death in the newspapers. Newspaper friends tell me there probably was no wire service obit. Strange.

With Glen Gray

After all those one-nighters with Bob Chester, I spent a pleasant six months with the Glen Gray (Casa Loma) band. We played ballrooms a week at a time, a theater tour, and also a booking at the Hotel Pennsylvania in New York. Herb Ellis had been the guitar player but there wasn't enough for Herb to do in the Casa Loma band. Herb is a beautiful, flashy soloist and it was easy to understand why he chose to work in a trio instead of a big band. Someone recommended me to Gray, and I'm glad he did, whoever it was.

Bobby Hackett had joined the band shortly before I did in 1945 and I met him on the bandstand, my chair being right next to the trumpet section. He introduced himself and I told him I knew, of course, who he was. "Nice to meet you," he said, and then he noticed my guitar. "Where's your motor?" he asked. I told him I didn't have one of those things. He told me he didn't like them either and we became good friends. Hackett played guitar as well as cornet.

In contrast to the fancy, amplified guitars many were beginning to use then, I suppose my old Gibson L-5, a somewhat battered and scratched-up working guitar, looked strange to some. But that guitar was damn near part of me and I was not amused when Ted McMichael of the Merry Macs, a singing group touring with the Casa Loma, said to me, "Gee, that's really a good sounding box and I do mean box. When are you going to take the nails out of it?" I said, "Sit down and drink your beer."

As is well known, the Casa Loma was the first cooperative band, and Henry Biagini was the band's leader before it became the Casa Loma. Casa Loma was the name of a Canadian nightclub, actually a castle brought from Europe stone by stone, where the band was supposed to play. But the Casa Loma club never opened. For some reason, the band members decided to call themselves the Casa Loma Orchestra, anyway. And I had been told by those who should know that the players in Biagini's band copied his arrangements before they all quit to form their own corporation. Alto saxophonist Glen Gray (real name Glen Gray Knoblaugh) was named president, manager Cork O'Keefe vice president, and tenor saxophonist Pat Davis secretary-treasurer, with stock going to seven other players. Could this be true? Could they have booted Biagini out and stolen his arrangements at the same time? Well, no one can check with Biagini now. In 1944 *Down Beat* reported that he was killed—like too many other musicians—in an automobile crash. He was returning to Detroit from a one-night stand in Lansing. The driver had fallen asleep at the wheel. Biagini was thirty-nine.

When I was with Glen Gray, a big man with huge hands, he and O'Keefe, who had his own booking office, simply split all the money. I have been told that no one got any of that corporation money except trumpet player Sonny Dunham, and he supposedly got $60,000. Trombonist Billy Rausch, one of the original stockholders and the player featured on the band's theme song, *Smoke Rings*, told me that he never got any corporation money. He said they told him there was no corporation money left because the band business was so bad and name bands were fading out. I do not pretend to know the financial details, but I have heard a number of former Casa Lomans say that the corporation was decidedly not what it was cracked up to be.

In any event, the Casa Loma band, historically, was a forerunner of the swing bands that followed it. Kids familiar with *Casa Loma Stomp, White Jazz, Blue Jazz, Black Jazz* and other Casa Loma tunes could understand Benny Goodman's music in a way they might not have understood it if there had been no Casa Loma. But when I played with Glen Gray, the band was not the attraction it had been in the middle 1930s. At one time it was probably the best white band, but then Benny and all the rest came along. In the 1950s, Gray had considerable success with a studio band playing some of the old Casa Loma arrangements on Capitol Records, and George T. Simon, in his book *The Big Bands,* says that Gray was offered substantial sums to appear publicly with a Casa Loma band again. But Glen preferred to remain at home in Peabody, Massachusetts, a decision this road veteran understands. Gray died of cancer in 1963.

When the tour with Glen Gray ended, I worked briefly, in the summer of 1946, with a band led by Bernie Mann that wasn't bad. It was strictly a dance band, violins included. Mann was only an amateur trumpet player, but he had good players. A handsome, Swedish-looking tenor saxophone player, George Dessinger, was wonderful. We also had Sonny Dunham on trumpet (his recording of *Memories of You* with the Casa Loma band helped to make him famous) and he doubled on trombone. Our trombone star was Walter Robertson and he played trumpet, too, so sometimes we had five trumpets. But that band didn't make it. I think the only decent job the band had was the one I worked at the Roosevelt Hotel. Mann's band replaced Guy Lombardo there that summer. It was, to be sure, a much better band than Lombardo's.

2

EXCITING NEW SOUNDS

With Stan Kenton

Playing with Stan Kenton's "progressive jazz" band was a great experience. The sounds! The incredible sounds!

When I worked with Kenton in 1947, we set up this way in ballrooms and theaters: Drummer Shelly Manne was in the center of the stage with bass player Eddie Safranski on his right. I was in front of Safranski and behind the five-man sax section. The brass section was to Shelly's left, and this *was* a brass section! Five trombones in the front row and six trumpets in the back row! What chops they all had. I have never heard anything like that brass section before or since. Not with Basie or anyone else. The brass sounds were awesome.

Safranski had a small amp beside him and behind me. I was on a riser one step lower than Safranski and his amp was right by my ear until he agreed to move it to his other side so that I wouldn't get all that constant electronic buzzing and humming. Safranski had another amp beside the trumpets because the trumpet players and trombone players on the end were so far away from Shelly Manne and Safranski that they couldn't hear either the bass or the drums. And they certainly couldn't hear my unamplified guitar. I couldn't hear it half the time myself.

Because the band was so loud, I once asked Stan why he even bothered to have a rhythm guitar player. He told me that he had to have a rhythm guitar because he was "not always able to play. I'm standing up so much of the time in front of the band. I need that extra rhythm."

Well, whether he truly did or not, and in most of his later bands he managed without guitar, I was glad he felt that way back then because playing in that Kenton band was a thrilling experience for me.

I joined the band when it was at the Adams Theater in Newark. Shelly Manne, an old friend and colleague from Will Bradley band days, called me one night from the Capitol Theater in Washington. He told me that guitar player Bob Ahearn had left Kenton and a replacement was needed right away. Apparently Shelly had recommended me. He explained that I could talk to someone about salary if I wanted to, but he felt certain that the price would be okay. It was.

I knew that the Kenton band was doing well while so many other big bands were foundering financially and ready to fold, so I agreed to make it, arriving the next morning at the Adams Theater in Newark.

The movie was almost over, the newsreel was about to begin, and the stage was dark except for pinlights on the music stands. Shelly was there to show me the music for the show and to make certain that Bob Ahearn had marked the cuts properly on the guitar charts. Sometimes a player will not mark all the cuts because he knows the music so well, playing it day after day.

So, after glancing through the arrangements for the show and getting a blue-jacket uniform, my first performance with the Kenton band was without rehearsal of any kind. I hadn't even laid eyes on Kenton until the show. A trumpet player or a sax player understandably hates to go in cold like that, but it's not so bad for a rhythm guitar player who needs to sight-read only chord symbols. Still, you have to be cautious. You don't want to be playing when you shouldn't be. Or not playing when you should be, which is what actually happened to me that day.

The lights went on, Kenton walked out, and we started to play *Artistry in Rhythm,* the Kenton theme based on the Daybreak Movement of Maurice Ravel's *Daphnis et Chloé.* I could see one trombone player out of the corner of my left eye and when the trombones began screeching and screaming I thought to myself *man, what a band!* The trombones were way up there (and I thought the whole brass section was playing)—Skip Layton in that trombone section could play higher on trombone than anyone I've ever heard—and then when the six trumpets started to shriek above the trombones I stopped playing, almost in fright. I had never, never heard anything like that before. Kenton looked at me and smiled. I started to play again.

After the show, I met Kenton and told him "I'm sorry I stopped playing during the theme. I had heard records of the band, *but!*" He understood.

Yes, the Kenton band was loud. But it was a marvelous band and I certainly did not agree with some of my swing band colleagues who kept putting the band down. During my time with Kenton in 1947, some excellent jazz musicians would ask me how I could stand to work in that "noisy band." One well-known player said, "Oh, so you're with Kenton now. My God, that's a silly band!" I told him that "if it's such a silly band, then you come and *try* to play with us some time. You'll find out how *silly* it is!"

I remember Ray McKinley, who had a good swinging band then, saying much the same thing. "I understand you're working with that noisemaker," he remarked to me between sets of a McKinley band performance. "Well," I told Ray, "everybody says that kind of stuff and you know you've got a good band here but your band couldn't even begin to play the Kenton book." McKinley had a sharp, precise, swinging trumpet section with Charlie Genduso playing lead, but Genduso could not have played lead trumpet in the Kenton band. "No one in your brass section could play one chart in Kenton's book," I added. "So it's hard," grumbled McKinley. "But that doesn't mean it swings."

Perhaps he had a point. And I know at least one member of the Kenton band agreed with McKinley. This was tenor saxophonist Vido Musso, a good friend of Stan's and a famous soloist long before he played with Kenton. Born in Sicily, he was the tenor soloist in Benny Goodman's 1936–38 band and was also featured with Gene Krupa, Harry James, and Woody Herman before joining Kenton. One time on the Kenton band bus, out of a clear blue sky, Vido turned to me and said, "Steve, you know what? This band stinks! We ain't swingin' nothin'!" And you couldn't argue with Vido when his mind was made up. If the band hadn't broken up, I figure Vido might have found other employment anyway. Indeed, a few months later, when I was with Boyd Raeburn and Kenton was about to reorganize his band, I remember *Down Beat* quoted Kenton as saying, "I will not take Vido back under any circumstances." So, Stan and Vido, though friends, had their differences. To me, Vido Musso was a delightful guy. Great player, too.

While with Kenton, I was completely thrilled by the very sound of the band and continually thought how lucky I was to hear that from the inside. Nearly two years later, listening to another Kenton band play some of the same charts in Carnegie Hall, where the acoustics are fine, I realized that the band sounded even better out front. I sat glued to my seat that night because the sound of the band was a revelation, almost unbelievable.

The Kenton "progressive jazz" band I worked with was no "silly band," but a great band with superior musicianship. It was a great pleasure to work with trombonists Kai Winding, Milt Bernhart (he sat next to Winding and used to gripe that he wasn't getting enough solos, and maybe he wasn't, but he was sitting with tough competition), Skip Layton (Skip was the one who did that compelling solo on Billie Holiday's famous *Travelin' Light* with a Paul Whiteman studio orchestra), bass trombonist Bart Varsallona, trumpet players Ray Wetzel (who had indefatigable lips, especially for such constant high range), Buddy Childers, and Chico Alvarez (a great jazz player), lead alto saxophonist Boots Mussulli (who did such a beautiful job on *Opus in Pastels*), baritone saxophonist Bob Gioga, and tenor saxophonists Red Dorris, Bob Cooper, and Musso.

Musso replaced Dorris while I was with the band after Red's mother became very ill, and singer June Christy became Mrs. Bob Cooper while I was with the band, too. June, inspired by Anita O'Day no doubt, was one of the best band singers and helped Kenton win many new followers.

It was a great band. So, maybe it wasn't a swing band. It certainly didn't sound like Count Basie or Benny Goodman. But the Kenton band certainly did swing when we played something like *Lover.* After all, a band such as Kenton's with fantastic harmonic embellishments cannot swing like a band using simpler chord patterns. The Kenton players were certainly able to swing as hard as those in Benny Goodman, Count Basie, or Woody Herman bands when given the opportunity.

I must note here, too, that I had no problems whatsoever with Kenton. The only guy like Kenton I've ever known in the music business was Richard Maltby. As trumpet player Jimmy Maxwell said of Maltby: "He's nicer to people than it's necessary to be." That can be said of Kenton, too.

I found Kenton to be an articulate, enthusiastic, hardworking, nice guy. And I always thought he was greatly underrated as a piano player (when I worked with him, his favorite piano player was Earl Hines). I suppose most people don't know how well Stan played the piano simply because he seldom featured his piano playing with the band, except in those elaborate concerto-to-end-all-concerto pieces.

I joined the Kenton band in February, 1947. We suffered through a blizzard in Milwaukee in March and the band broke up in Kansas City. Kenton had a tremendous payroll—over $5,000 a week—but was solidly in the black. In those days, Kenton was big box office wherever he played. When the band broke up, I understood that Kenton had to give up the band because of overwork and doctor's advice that he was heading for a nervous breakdown. He soon reorganized for a southern tour—I was not on that tour—but his health forced him to disband again after a week or so. Kenton forfeited $150,000 in guarantees for dates booked in advance. He did not reorganize again for five months. By that time I was with Boyd Raeburn. Stan wrote me a nice note explaining that he planned to use Brazilian guitarist Laurindo Almeida, who plays wonderful concert guitar, finger style (no pick). Almeida is not a rhythm man but became nationally known as a soloist playing with Kenton.

I will always cherish my time with Kenton's band. Anyone who puts Stan Kenton or his music down gets an argument from me.

Like anyone who ever knew the man, I was distressed to hear about his skull fracture in 1977, which required brain surgery, was cheered when he had recovered sufficiently to take a band on the road again in 1978, and deeply saddened at the news of his death due to a stroke—brought about, I assume, by that skull fracture from which he never fully recovered—in August, 1979. I was told that the skull fracture resulted from a mugging in an unprotected parking area underneath a building in Boston.

With Boyd Raeburn

After playing with Kenton, I was soon with the Boyd Raeburn band. Boyd's band was just as wild, and maybe even more "progressive" than Kenton's band. Since I had moved from Kenton to Raeburn, one guy told me, "That's like going out of the frying pan *into* the frying pan!"

When the Kenton band broke up everyone went to the West Coast. But my home was New York City, so they gave me a train ticket in Kansas City. I had been home only about a week, doing nothing, when Irving Kluger, the drummer, called. He was going with the new Boyd Raeburn band and thought I might be interested, too. It seems strange that within a few weeks so many bands broke up, including Kenton, Woody Herman, Tommy Dorsey, and Benny Goodman. Raeburn was determined to get the best players he could find, money being no problem thanks to his wealthy backer, Stillman Pond, a West Coast real estate man. The Raeburn venture was Pond's second attempt at being a band "angel." His first try flopped when a band called the King Guion Double-Rhythm band couldn't make it. Pond, a big jolly guy, sank more than $100,000 into the 1947 Raeburn band.

From Kenton's band, Raeburn got trombonists Milt Bernhart and Bart Varsallona and me. From Herman, he picked up trumpet players Pete Candoli and Conrad Gozzo. Trumpet player Bernie Glow had worked with so many big bands, I forgot just what band he came directly from. Our lead trombone player, Dick Noel, who played beautifully, came from Tommy Dorsey's band, as I recall. And we had a terrific lead alto player, Jerry Sanfino, who had been with Alvino Rey. Clarinetist Buddy DeFranco, who certainly could play, worked with the band later, too, coming from Tommy Dorsey.

This was a *big* big band, bigger than Kenton's band except for the brass section. Most bands then were fourteen or fifteen pieces, but Raeburn had twenty-two players including seven saxophone players who doubled on other reed instruments. One was Sam Spumberg, a veteran Broadway show musician who was hired because he could play English horn as well as bass saxophone, flute, and piccolo. He was a most valuable man in this band and he must have been paid well. I do know that Gozzo was getting $300 a week and Candoli $250 a week, excellent money then. And along with the seven reeds, we had two French horns with one of the French horn players coming directly from the Minneapolis Symphony Orchestra, a young lady playing harp, a bassoon player, plus four rhythm and eight brass. The bassoon player, Shirley Thompson, was a Broadway show musician with a passion for baseball. At that time he was compiling an encyclopedia of baseball players. Raeburn played tenor, baritone, and soprano sax as well as the seldom-heard bass sax, but he played only occasionally with the band because few of the arrangements included him.

I had recorded with Raeburn in 1945, playing George Handy arrangements with a terrific group including Ike Carpenter, Shelly Manne, Al Cohn, Walter Robertson, Hal McKusick, Trummy Young, Oscar Pettiford, Stan Fishelson, and Dizzy Gillespie. The result was the album entitled *Boyd Meets Stravinsky.*

I respected Boyd's approach to music. He may have started as a society music bandleader in Chicago in the 1930s playing Mickey Mouse junk, but by 1945 he wanted only the best arrangements and the best players he could find. Johnny Richards wrote almost all of the charts for the 1947–48 Raeburn band although Boyd did use some of the pieces George Handy had done for him in 1945. Many musicians and critics raved about the band, noting that some of our music brought Stravinsky, Bartok, Debussy, and Ravel to mind. But though we made it artistically, the band did not succeed commercially.

I remember one night we worked a job at the University of Virginia in Charlottesville. It was homecoming weekend or something. Our band was in a small gymnasium. Another band led by Johnny Long was the big attraction and was in the huge, main gym. Long played the violin left-handed and his band played predictable, nice, sweet dance music. After we played our first set, the kids were screaming for more. They weren't dancing, just listening. In addition to the excellent charts by Richards, we dug into George Handy's *Boyd Meets Stravinsky* and *Dalvatore Sali* and some of Handy's even wilder things. Word got around the campus that there was true musical excitement in the small gym and soon the place was so packed that fire department and security people refused to let anyone else in. The windows to the gym were open and kids were climbing the gym's walls to listen through the windows. Half of Johnny Long's musicians had walked in during their intermission and they told us that there was hardly anyone in their big gym, just a tiny handful dancing. But that night the Johnny Long band was paid $4,000 and the Raeburn band was paid only $800.

Boyd Raeburn's band was exciting and innovative and musically hip, but it couldn't earn enough money to pay the salaries of the twenty-two musicians, some of the best in the country. Stillman Pond had to make up the difference and eventually he simply got tired of doing so and the band broke up. Pond had plenty of money and he believed in the band. But enough became enough for him and I guess he figured he'd be better off investing in a Broadway show or polo ponies or almost anything but a first-class big band. We folded in June, 1948.

Raeburn later had a fourteen-piece band, cutting down his arrangements for twenty-two pieces somehow, and did work the Paramount Theater with some "star" singer whose name escapes me. But soon—like an old soldier no one cares enough about—his band just faded away.

Boyd and his beautiful wife, Ginny Powell, who sang with his band—and she could *sing,* too—moved to Nassau in the Bahamas about 1950 where Boyd became a hotel manager. But Ginny caught hepatitis in Nassau and she died there in 1959.

Boyd had two small daughters and—soon after Ginny's death—he moved to New Orleans where he ran a furniture store. I suppose most all of his customers had no idea he had once led one of the nation's most original big jazz bands. Then a horrible automobile accident in 1963 left him with serious internal injuries. After a long hospital stay, he was able to return to work but he was never healthy again, and the internal injuries finally killed him.

When he died in 1966 at the age of fifty-two I had to learn about it through the grapevine. I saw no obit about Boyd Raeburn in the newspapers nor did any of my friends. I found that curious and sad.

Boyd Raeburn was a good guy and a sharp businessman. Too bad his band, a great one in many ways, never made it. It should have.

3

THE KING AND I

With Benny's 1953 Big Band

I've worked with many wonderful jazz clarinet players—Edmond Hall, Hank D'Amico, Artie Shaw, Pee Wee Russell, Fazola, Buddy DeFranco, and Peanuts Hucko included—but nobody played like Benny Goodman. In my book, as in many other books, he is the number one jazz clarinet player of all time, no question.

His playing, like that of all great "hot" players from Louis Armstrong on, had heart, emotional wallop, passion. He also had a gorgeous sound in all registers, read like an IBM machine, and he sounded like no one but himself. And Lord knows he could swing. He played joy, happiness, as few ever have.

Happiness. What we all seek. Long before I joined the Goodman band I remember Bud Freeman telling me this: "It's a well-known fact that no human being in the history of the world has even been completely happy. The closest I've ever come to it was the first night I played with Benny Goodman's band."

I remembered Bud's remark when I went to audition for Benny's band, and although working for Benny was not always predictable—he could be strange at times—I came to feel the same way. It was a thrill working with his big bands and small groups, as I did off and on for four years.

Yes, like everyone else who has worked for Benny, I have my Benny stories—when you were talking to Benny he would sometimes fluff you off and act dopey or say the damndest things with a straight face—but as Bobby Hackett said, "I think any guy who plays as well as Benny does is entitled to a few eccentricities."

In March, 1953, I was living in New York City, not working steady any-where—playing pickup jobs, recording with small groups, taking any kind of job where rhythm guitar was needed—when I read in *Down Beat* magazine that Benny Goodman was going to get a band together, his first band in five years. Benny had been concentrating on classical music, but the pop-ularity of his 1938 Carnegie Hall concert recordings, released in 1950, and his more exciting 1937–38 broadcast recordings released later proved that there was an enormous Goodman audience eager to hear a Goodman band playing the old arrangements, and I guess Benny felt the urge to swing again with a big band.

I noticed that John Hammond, the jazz promoter and record producer who became Benny's brother-in-law in 1942, was to manage the band's six-week tour that was to include Louis Armstrong's small group on the program. So I called John, whom I had known since 1939—I first met him in The Famous Door on 52d Street when I was with Will Bradley's band—and asked him if the guitar chair was set in Benny's new band yet. John told me that guitarists would be auditioned soon and that he'd have Benny give me a ring. He added that if I still played the way I did with Freddie Slack's band—John had heard me with Slack in New Orleans when he was in the Army stationed at Camp Plauche—I'd be perfect for Benny.

I figured it was kind of John to say that but thought little more about my chances of auditioning for Goodman's new "all-star" band.

A few days later my rooming house landlady woke me up in the morning for a phone call. Half asleep after a late night, I grabbed the phone and the caller said, "Hello, this is Benny Goodman." Figuring it might be a friend being funny, I said, "And this is Buffalo Bill."

"No, no," the voice said, "this is Benny Goodman. John Hammond asked me to call you. I understand you might be interested in auditioning for my new band."

I said yes and he asked me what bands I had played in. I told him Will Bradley and Ray McKinley, Teddy Powell, Glen Gray, Artie Shaw—and with the mention of Shaw's name he said, "Oh, really?"—Stan Kenton, Boyd Raeburn, and I named a few others.

"Sounds good," he said, "I'll listen to you." Benny, I was to discover, was not easily impressed. He told me his band was rehearsing at two o'clock that afternoon at Nola studios on 57th Street, if I could make it. I could make it.

Upon arrival, I discovered that six other guitarists had already auditioned and had apparently failed to satisfy Benny, and that Hy White, who played with Woody Herman for many years, would be next, then me.

Hy, a marvelous guy and a fine player too, told me he came along "just for the ride." He said that because of his successful teaching practice he probably wouldn't be able to travel with the band even if he got the job. I wondered about that. In any event he didn't get the job.

As I entered the studio I noticed many famous jazz players I had never met, including Teddy Wilson, Ziggy Elman, Willie Smith, and Vernon Brown. One I had worked with, Charlie Shavers, was there too, as was Georgie Auld, whom I knew slightly, and Gene Krupa. I had worked with Gene three nights in Tommy Dorsey's band. Man, I thought, all these great musicians, and I'll be playing with them all at once. But it wasn't to be that way. Not right away, anyhow.

I went to the guitar chair and Benny said, "Everybody relax except the guitar and saxophones. Get out *Roll 'Em*," he added, telling us that was number forty-seven in the book or whatever number it was.

There was no bass to hide behind, no drummer to latch onto, just me and four saxes. Benny played the brass fills on clarinet. As I came to learn, he seemed to know all his old arrangements by heart, and *Roll 'Em*, written by Mary Lou Williams for his band in 1937, was one of his favorites. Even with my background and experience, I felt a little nervous at the beginning, but as we played I noticed Benny nodding his head to John Hammond, who was sitting back in the corner, and I felt good about that.

After we finished, Benny said he liked my playing and asked if I could stay and rehearse with the band or if I had to be somewhere else soon. "We'll be out of here by five," he said. Of course, I could stay.

He didn't introduce me to anybody but I was apparently Benny Goodman's guitar player. Working in the rhythm section that day with Gene Krupa, Israel Crosby, and Teddy Wilson, and with Benny swinging right beside me, was some kind of happiness.

After rehearsal, he made it official. Would you like to be with the band? *Would I?* He told me to go to Willard Alexander's office and talk to Irv Dinkin about money. I'd known Irv for years. Benny paid well and put you right on salary when the band was rehearsing. This band rehearsed about two weeks, as I remember, and you could gig at night for extra money if you wanted, as some of our band members did. When you went, say, on a fourteen-week tour with Benny you signed a contract. It protected him and it protected you. He couldn't fire you unless you did something god-awful and you couldn't give notice. It was a fair system all around, I think.

During this rehearsal period with Goodman I was in Jim 'n Andy's bar one evening (I'd say the four major watering holes for musicians in Manhattan at that time were Charlie's Tavern, Junior's Bar, Joe Harbor's Spotlight Cafe, and Jim 'n Andy's) and my old Will Bradley band buddy Felix Giobbe, at ABC staff then, barrels in. He leaned on me, wrapped a huge arm around my shoulder in something like a bearlike grip and said: "Hey, I hear you're playing with Benny. Why in the hell do you want to play with him?" I explained, "It's been a life's ambition, Felix." "Man," he said, "don't you know Jews can't swing?" I knew he was putting me on but I replied, "What?" Felix said, "Now Hank D'Amico, he can play! And Al Gallodoro, he eats a clarinet for breakfast. When he's playing charts in the studios he not only plays every note he even plays the part at the bottom that says Passantino Brand!" All this was delivered with a straight face, as if he meant it. "Good luck, kid, I'll see you around," he wound up. That was Giobbe. His attitude was that if it's not Italian, whatever it is, it's not the best. And he was a master of the put-on, too. (Jim 'n Andy's, on 48th Street west of Sixth Avenue, is long gone now, demolished in the late 1960s along with book and music stores on 48th between Sixth and Seventh Avenues to make way for still more dull, tall, glass buildings. Some call that progress.)

In addition to the rhythm section of Krupa, Wilson, Crosby, and me, that 1953 band was composed of Willie Smith and Clint Neagley on alto sax, Georgie Auld and Sol Schlinger on tenor sax, trumpeters Ziggy Elman, Charlie Shavers, and Al Stewart, trombonists Vernon Brown and Rex Peer, and singer Helen Ward, who was with Benny's first band and came out of retirement to rejoin him.

Rex Peer was a newcomer to big-time jazz. Benny had heard him at a jam session at Iowa State University after Benny had played there one evening. He told Rex then that if he ever came to New York to call him. He did, and at the proper time, since he called when Benny happened to be putting together this 1953 band. But Rex Peer's name in the program, and subsequently in *Down Beat* magazine, was printed "Ray Peet," and he was terribly upset about that. He had wanted to send the magazine back to his parents in Iowa. A fine player, Rex Peer, and he learned a lot from Urbie Green, who played beside him in a later Goodman band at the Waldorf-Astoria.

Ziggy Elman had been on the West Coast for a long time and certainly didn't need the money. He owned a liquor store in Springfield, Massachusetts, he and his brother shared ownership in a carpet and rug business in Atlantic City, and Ziggy was working regularly playing his horn in Las Vegas. But he must have wanted to play those old Goodman charts again because he made the trip all the way from California by train to rejoin Benny. Ziggy was afraid to fly. Another reason for his enthusiasm was Benny's offer of $750 a week plus hotel expenses.

One of the dates we had on this tour was at the famous old Academy of Music in Philadelphia—pigeon dirt on the outside and marvelous acoustics on the inside. This show in Philly ended before midnight and a few of us went out for a drink and something to eat. After coming back to the hotel (the St. James, then a transient hotel, the kind that has a little hole in the rug next to the bed where people step year after year and open transoms above the doors), I was walking down the corridor toward my room when I heard the unmistakable singing of Ziggy Elman. This was just after Mario Lanza had made it big singing *Be My Love*. Ziggy, obviously juicing a little, was singing Lanza's hit song loudly, something like Lanza, but with a change in the title line. "Be My GUE-E-E-ST!" sang Ziggy.

Having been on the West Coast for a good many years, Ziggy had many friends and relatives from Atlantic City and Philadelphia he hadn't seen for some time, and more than a dozen of them were in Ziggy's room that night. Ziggy had bought a couple of cases for the occasion. He insisted I be his guest, too. And I was.

Ziggy was a wild, wonderful guy, and could he play! A lot of jazz critics— but not leaders such as Goodman or Tommy Dorsey—have always underrated Ziggy and Harry James. Ziggy especially. Don't ask me why. Well, Ziggy's gone now. Dead at fifty-four in 1968. Benny had discovered him playing in Alex Bartha's house band at Atlantic City's Steel Pier in 1936 when Ziggy was eighteen or nineteen years old. Though featured on alto sax with Bartha, he was playing lead trumpet when Benny heard him. Needing a good trumpet player because of the departure of Zeke Zarchy due to a bum lip, he certainly found one in Ziggy.

Clint Neagley, a fine player, was hired for lead alto in Benny's new band, but when Benny found out he could get Willie Smith, who led that wonderful Jimmie Lunceford reed section in the 1930s, Clint moved over to third alto, probably for the same money. He didn't seem to mind the switch from lead alto at all. "Man," he said, "I love to play third alto in this band just to hear Willie Smith blow!"

But all was not bliss with Benny on that 1953 tour. There were problems between Benny and Louis Armstrong, which have been detailed neatly by John Hammond in his 1978 autobiography *John Hammond on Record*. Armstrong stayed on stage much too long to suit Benny, Benny felt the tour didn't need Armstrong, Armstrong felt he didn't need Goodman. I remember problems during rehearsal, too.

The Armstrong band had been working at night and rehearsal began at ten o'clock in the morning. Louis and his five band members—prominent musicians all, namely Joey Bushkin, Cozy Cole, Arvell Shaw, Barney Bigard, and Trummy Young—were still sitting around at two in the afternoon one day with Louis grumbling to Benny, "Hey, when do we play?"

Benny replied, "I'll get to you in a moment, Pops," and Louis put him down. I forget precisely what Louis said—something like when Benny was a kid, in short pants, I'd let him sit in and play with my band in Chicago and now he is trying to upstage me—but George Auld, playing peacemaker, went over and patted Louis on the shoulder, saying, "Don't, please, don't worry about it." Louis kept saying that he didn't need to go on any tour with Goodman because he could arrange his own tour. But it was ironed out, more or less.

And there was a far more serious problem with Benny in 1953. Remember, this band was the first he'd had in five years. He'd been playing with symphony orchestras all over the country—billed as *Benjamin* Goodman—and had been using a legitimate embouchure after study with Reginald Kell, the famous English classical clarinetist. I'm told, too, that Kell got mad at Benny for some reason and booked himself into the same places and with the same symphony orchestras Benny played with and cut him to ribbons—on legitimate clarinet, that is. In any event, the legitimate or "double" embouchure is much different from the single embouchure that Benny and just about all jazz players use. With legitimate you cover both sets of teeth with your lips and the mouthpiece is held between both lips instead of between the lower lip and the upper teeth. Legitimate produces a purer sound. Benny's problem in 1953 was that he would switch from one embouchure to the other without realizing it. Because of this, sometimes he'd try to hit a high note and nothing would come out of the clarinet. I think he realized that everybody in that 1953 band was playing well except himself. His playing was all mixed up somehow.

John Hammond said to me one night, "Look, we've got to do something. Benny is liable to never play again. We can't let that happen."

"I'm with you, John," I said, "but what can I do? I don't know the man that way. I have absolutely no influence over him. I hardly even know him."

I have no idea how, but somehow Benny snapped out of it. He conquered the embouchure problem and whatever else was bothering him. There is, I think, much truth to the view expressed by John Hammond in his book that "Benny is such a perfectionist, so uniformly flawless as a musician, that even the slightest deviation from the norm is immediately noticeable."

Benny did not complete this 1953 tour. Arriving in Boston from Providence, he collapsed twice due to an indigestion problem and sheer exhaustion. It was first thought to have been a heart attack. When he collapsed the first time, a fire department rescue squad was able to revive him after an hour and forty minutes using an oxygen tank. Gene Krupa took over leadership of the band in Boston.

Even without Benny, we drew capacity crowds everywhere. After all, there were many big jazz names in Benny's band and Louis Armstrong had an all-star group, too. One night during the tour, at the Cleveland Auditorium, I saw record producer Norman Granz backstage before the performance. The curtains were closed and the house was packed. Firemen had checked the standing-room-only area for balcony safety. But Norman, who booked part of the tour along with Willard Alexander and Joe Glaser, said, "Benny should be here! He's not too sick to continue the tour!" I looked at Granz, who was dressed like a king and was as rich as a king, and asked him, "Where would you put the extra people that Benny would have drawn, anyway? Do you think you're losing money?" Norman didn't answer. He just stood there, wringing his hands and tearing up a program. Money-mad people always have been off my list. Even before Benny left the tour, both John Hammond and Gene Krupa had told me that Benny was sick and had been advised by doctors to abandon the rest of the tour.

With the Goodman Sextet in 1954

By the summer of 1954 I was with a new Goodman sextet at the Basin Street club in New York, and he was playing extremely well. This was the best small group I've worked with regularly: Benny, Charlie Shavers on trumpet, pianist Mel Powell, bass player Israel Crosby, drummer Morey Feld, and me.

I got a congratulatory telegram the night the sextet opened at Basin Street. Normally only leaders get such telegrams. It was from Mary Selgren, a very nice, very clever girl I knew and loved dearly. I had worked with her for a while in a custom tailoring shop. The telegram read: "HERE'S A WARM HAND ON YOUR OPENING. LOVE, MARY."

Benny had this same group in Las Vegas that fall at the Last Frontier Hotel. This was the old Last Frontier Hotel (they've built a new one since), the last boots-and-saddle-looking place in Vegas. It had Indian blankets on the bannisters. It didn't look like all the Hiltons. It had a character of its own.

One day, Benny, Mel Powell, and I were talking out in front of the hotel and Benny had an appointment to see a Cadillac salesman. So the guy came up and tried to sell a fancy new Cadillac convertible to Benny. The salesman carefully explained all the car's gimmickry. You didn't even need to push a button to put the top up. If you had the top down and it started to rain, a water sensor automatically put the top up. It was beautiful. Benny drove it down the road and back, then thanked the salesman but told him he didn't need a new car. And the guy said, "Well, what are you driving now?" Benny told him he had an Oldsmobile 88 that was about two years old and a Ford station wagon that his maid used for shopping and picking up the kids after school. The guy looked bewildered. "You're Benny Goodman and you drive an Oldsmobile 88? A man in your position should have something like this gorgeous Cadillac!"

"Well now, that's where you're wrong," said Benny. "You see, young guys from New York or Chicago, singers or screenwriters or whatever, making about $1000 or $1500 a week, nobody knows them and they come to Hollywood and maybe *they* need something like your Cadillac so that when they pull up in front of the Brown Derby restaurant people figure they've *got* to be somebody. But not me. I can get out of a Fiat and everybody will say, 'Look, there's Benny Goodman!' So, you see, I don't need a car like yours in my position."

The salesman had no answer to that and didn't even attempt one.

It must have been several years later before Benny bought another car. It was a Cadillac but it wasn't a convertible, just a big black sedan.

And here's a story that tells more about the man than most Benny stories do. It happened when we were in a rehearsal hall on Broadway. Between tunes, Benny took a half-dollar out of his pocket and told the bandboy to run out and get some coffee, but he dropped the half-dollar and it rolled somewhere out of sight. Benny asked Mel Powell to look under the piano and he asked me to look under the radiator. We couldn't find the coin. After being down on my hands and knees, I simply wanted to give Benny fifty cents from my own pocket and say, here, Benny, here's half a buck, let's forget it. But you couldn't do that with Benny. As Mel said to me then, you don't do that because he'd take your half-dollar, the kid would get the coffee, then after the rehearsal was over and everyone else had gone, Benny would probably come back and get down on the floor and look for the lost half-dollar. He doesn't mind going out and spending $100 for dinner for his wife and himself, he pays his musicians well and he will *give* you something, but to lose something! Mel said then that because he was poverty stricken as a child in a Chicago ghetto, he can't stand to lose even a dime, and despite all the money he has made, he will always be poor in spirit. (Benny was one of twelve children of a poor sweatshop tailor. He was ten years old when he first put lip to clarinet mouthpiece in a neighborhood synagogue that offered music lessons for a quarter. When the synagogue was forced to end its music program for lack of money, Goodman and two of his brothers joined the band at Hull House, the famous settlement house founded by social reformer Jane Addams. The rest of the Goodman rags to riches story is well known: A musician's musician as a teenager with the Ben Pollack band, and a busy recording studio musician and jazz solo whiz long before he became a show business sensation in the mid-1930s while in his late twenties.

Related story: In Vegas I was in a small restaurant one night with Mel, and Benny and his wife Alice were in the next booth. We had just finished our last show around 1:30, and this restaurant, called the '49er, had a special breakfast from midnight until 8 a.m.—two eggs, ham, bacon, or sausage, toast and coffee for only forty-nine cents. A good deal. We were all talking and suddenly Benny said, "It's after two o'clock and I need some sleep, I'll see you both tomorrow." After Benny and Alice left, Mel said, "Now you know why he's going back to the hotel so quickly, don't you? It's so he can get enough sleep to get up in time to have breakfast here again before eight o'clock. After eight, breakfast is a dollar and a half!"

Benny could be fun, Benny could be kind, but Benny could do some strange, inexplicable things. Mel Powell said the band stopped at an all-night diner one night in 1941 and he happened to be sharing a booth with Benny. Benny ordered a ham steak and as he was about to put catsup on it, the bottle cap dropped on the middle of his ham steak. Benny didn't mention it, just kept on talking and carving around the cap. When he was finished, there was a tiny piece of ham steak left on his plate with a bottle cap on top of it. That's Benny.

While we were in Vegas for a month at the Last Frontier, one time paychecks for the five band members were about two days late. Benny said the accountant must have goofed or something and that the checks should arrive in a day or two, and asked if anybody wanted to draw any pay in advance. He said, to all of us, "Need any money? Whatever you need. I've got credit here." Charlie Shavers said he'd take $50 to gamble a bit, and I said I'd take $20 in case of anything. We all sent our excess bread to a bank in New York.

Two days later the checks arrived from New York and that evening Benny handed out the checks after the first show. This was about ten o'clock. Benny then came out to the bar where I was sitting with Mel Powell and Morey Feld. He pulled me aside and asked, "Hey, have you got that twenty I loaned you the other day?" I had about five bucks in my pocket. I said no, I didn't.

"Okay, forget about it," he said, "after all, you needed the money and I loaned it to you."

"Wait a minute," I said, "do you need it right now? I just got my paycheck."

"Do I need it right now? Do I *need* it?" he asked with sarcasm.

I got so damn mad I quickly cashed the check at the club's bank, came back and said, "Hey, man, here's your twenty!"

Benny could be strange sometimes. Especially about money, as Mel Powell contends.

We worked a month in Vegas, playing two shows a night, forty minutes each, that's all. The rest of the time there was a big dance band and dancing girls, too. We played many of Benny's famous sextet hits—*Slipped Disc, Air Mail Special* for example—and Benny liked jam sessions, too, calling tunes on the spot. It was never boring. And Benny always had great confidence in his players. If someone told him he wasn't sure he knew the chord changes to a certain tune, or the bridge, or whatever, Benny would say "oh sure you do" and then go ahead and kick it off. And though you may have worried about what would happen when it comes to that bridge you thought you didn't know, it all worked out okay somehow. He was extremely casual about that kind of thing. He had the idea that since you are working with Benny Goodman, you must know all the tunes, or something. Benny had great confidence in his players.

Mel Powell, a marvelous piano player who left jazz to study with Paul Hindemith and teach composition at Yale, and later became dean of music at the California Institute of the Arts, is a charming, intellectual wit. He told me that all those piano-shaped or kidney-shaped swimming pools in Vegas weren't for swimming at all, but were made for women to sit around, in mink and sunglasses. And he's right. It was fun hanging around with philosopher Mel in Vegas, swimming in the oblong, old-fashioned pool at the Last Frontier.

One day beside the pool we were watching the construction of another hotel right next door. A huge crane was lifting and placing tall girders for the riveters and was surrounding itself on all sides with those girders. I asked Mel how they'd get the crane out of there without taking it completely apart. He said they'd probably leave it there "so people could drop a quarter into a slot and the crane will pick up a mink coat or a Cadillac and drop it down a chute to them." Yeah, large-scale Las Vegas!

Since Powell studied with Hindemith, plays complex formal music beautifully, and has written many serious pieces, I asked him why he never puts any of that stuff into his jazz playing. I suggested his jazz work could be a lot more complicated than that of the beboppers and the progressive jazz people. Mel simply said, "Oh, no, you don't do that. It isn't fair. And anyway, it wouldn't swing."

Like Goodman, Mel was a jazz whiz even as a teenager. Benny played with Bix Beiderbecke at fourteen and by sixteen was a star in Ben Pollack's band. Mel had a Dixieland band at twelve, graduated from high school at fourteen, and by sixteen the tall, blue-eyed blond had changed his name from Epstein and was playing with Bobby Hackett and Muggsy Spanier. By eighteen, in 1941, he was with Benny's band and sextet, making $500 a week, great money for any sideman then. The story goes that Muggsy Spanier was so mad at Benny for taking Mel from his band that he made a record that had "FEATURING BENNY GOODMAN" on the label. Muggsy had found another clarinet player in New York named Benny Goodman.

Mel wrote a number of fascinating pieces for the Goodman band, including *The Earl, Clarinade,* and *Mission to Moscow.* And Benny's popular version of *Jersey Bounce* was arranged by Mel. He is certainly one of the greatest of all jazz piano players. Ever. He's been married to famous movie actress Martha Scott (Emily in Thornton Wilder's 1938 Broadway hit *Our Town,* and who became a movie star in the 1940 film version of that play) since 1946. Who says movie stars never stay married to the same guy?

Mel won the Pulitzer prize for music in 1990 with a concerto for two pianos and orchestra entitled *Duplicates.* If there were a Pulitzer for jazz piano, he would or *should* have won that long ago. Mel could sound like Fats Waller one minute, Earl Hines the next, and then like Teddy Wilson. Wilson once said, while listening to an old Goodman small-group record, "Well, that's either Mel Powell playing like me or me!"

I hadn't seen Mel since 1959 until I went to hear a program of his music at Washington's Kennedy Center in October, 1990. The eight compositions indicated Mel's versatility, since they were composed for a small orchestra, a string quartet, two pianos, five wind instruments, violin and harp, solo flute, and solo percussionist. For me, this was music that made Stravinsky seem conservative. It must be extremely difficult to play, but the musicians, who were students, teachers, and alumni of the California Institute of the Arts, certainly seemed to meet the challenge. A *Washington Post* review by Mark Carrington said that "Powell writes music that is rigorously disciplined in an academic sense yet accessible. Highbrow music, if you will, without the frown." He also said, "Each [piece] was a joyous assemblage of melodic line and coloration, exactly the kind of material one might expect to hear from a former arranger for the great Benny Goodman band." I guess so, but recalling his writing for Benny, surely Mel is involved in a completely different kind of musical activity now. For example, here's a sample line by Mel from his program notes, describing one movement of his *Divertimento for Five Winds* as a "rondo-finale reflecting the jazziness of Hindemith-Prokofiev-Stravinsky reflecting on Mozart reflecting on Haydn." Got that?

I had arranged to see Mel backstage. He was as upbeat and witty as ever but looked quite different, with long, white hair at sixty-seven. He couldn't believe that it had been thirty-one years since we had played together. Someone asked him if he were going to perform that night. Mel said he didn't play much any more because of a touch of arthritis in his right hand. Maybe he simply didn't want to play and was finding a polite excuse. I know that a week earlier his wife Martha told me on the phone that Mel "plays all the time." I believe Martha. And I'm glad there's no arthritic touch in his left hand, since he's left-handed. Being left-handed, Mel said, was why it was easy for him to learn stride piano as a kid. Mel's powerful left hand was a distinguishing feature of his jazz playing.

Since my last recording session with Mel in 1959, he became chairman of music composition at Yale (succeeding his own teacher, Paul Hindemith), began the Electronic Music Studio at Yale, became founding dean of the School of Music at the California Institute of the Arts, then served as provost of that school, which was created twenty-odd years ago with the help of money from Walt Disney.

As for Mel's view of Benny's playing, he summed it up this way to writer James Lincoln Collier (for Collier's book *Benny Goodman and the Swing Era*): "Benny was one of the most incredible players. It wasn't just that his own improvisation was marvelous, the spirit, the verve, the vitality, even humor he played with, but the sheer technical mastery. The only thing comparable from a technical point of view would be Art Tatum."

Benny wasn't much of a drinker, although Bucky Pizzarelli, the fine guitar player who worked with Benny often during the 1970s, told me that on a few occasions Benny had a few belts before shows and really came on cooking. "Swinging like hell," said Bucky.

And I remember one drinking incident with Charlie Shavers, a great trumpet player and delightful guy, that annoyed Charlie when a few words from Benny might have solved the problem.

Charlie and I had the same dressing room in Vegas, and Benny made a habit of dropping in, opening up Charlie's trumpet case, where he knew there would always be a fifth of Scotch, and taking a belt. I think he did it to be funny. But it wasn't funny to Charlie. "Dammit," he said to me, "let him buy his own booze, he's got millions of dollars."

So after about a week of this, Benny came in with a bottle of Scotch. He said to Charlie, "Here, I've been drinking a little of your Scotch, so take this." It was a brand Charlie had never heard of. I'd never heard of it either. Charlie wouldn't take it. He thought it was cheap stuff. He told Benny, "You drink your Scotch and I'll drink mine, and we'll all be friends." Benny laughed and walked away. I told John Hammond about this incident later and John said it was undoubtedly one of the unusual British brands that Benny liked and the fifth probably cost him about forty-five dollars (remember, this was a 1955 price), anything but cheap stuff. Benny had taken no more than five or six drinks from Charlie's bottle, knew Charlie was getting steamed up about it, and was only trying to settle him down. He could have told Charlie what that bottle of Scotch cost, since Charlie thought it was cheap stuff. But he didn't.

Charlie Shavers didn't think much of Vegas. He said there was a kind of black veto all over, like the Deep South, and they didn't want blacks in the casinos. The first night we were there I said to Charlie, "Let's go to the bar and have a taste." He didn't want to go. "They don't want me at that bar," he said. "I don't believe it," I said, "this is Las Vegas." I finally convinced him to join us at the bar. After all, he was in the Goodman Sextet and he had the powder blue jacket uniform on. He had a drink there but he didn't like being there. He felt a draft, and he never went to that bar again. He'd stay in his dressing room between shows, and after the gig he'd go to black clubs that were open all night. He said the rest of Vegas "might as well be Atlanta." I was amazed! I always thought Vegas was wide open to everyone.

Only Benny and Mel Powell stayed in the Last Frontier. The union doesn't want band members to stay in a hotel where they work because the union believes it's something like a kickback, since the hotel pays the band. But Mel wouldn't go for that. He didn't care what the union thought. "I'm going to stay in the hotel where I'm working and that's it."

Tour of the Orient

The Goodman band's tour of the Orient in late 1956 into early 1957 was memorable. But it got off to a frantic start because someone running the tour schedule from Willard Alexander's booking office had forgotten the international date line.

It's not as if we didn't know we were crossing the international date line when we crossed it. I remember that when we did drummer Mousey Alexander, a funny guy, said: "Gee, it's Tuesday. Monday never happened. Yesterday never took place. I'm not married. Where are the stewardesses?"

But we thought we were arriving the day before we were to play in Bangkok for the King of Siam and dignitaries from other countries at the summer palace. Upon arrival we discovered we were to play that night. Muriel Zuckerman, Benny's longtime secretary, ran around in a tizzy collecting band jackets for pressing and somehow managed to get those wrinkled jackets pressed in time (a Goodman band does not appear in wrinkled jackets!) and a few hours later we were on stage, though hardly recovered from thirty hours of flying in piston-engine planes.

The twenty-eight-year-old king of Thailand, Bhumibol Adulyadej (officially King Rama IX), and his beautiful twenty-year-old bride, Queen Sirikit, sat in large chairs in front of the audience. At the end of the concert, the king came to shake Benny's hand and congratulate the band. He loved jazz and in fact played fairly decent clarinet. He spoke good English, of course. I say of course because he was born in Boston while his father was studying at Harvard. Because he was suddenly king, he returned to Siam (Thailand) from school in Switzerland after his elder brother died. Someone told me he didn't want to be king, but had no choice because the King of Siam was a divine-right ruler. As the king was in front of the band, Benny said, "I have something for you." The king looked at the package, smiled, and said, "I think I know what this is but I'm not supposed to open any gifts in public." Then he explained that, in this instance, he was going to forget such protocol. He found what he had expected, a clarinet case with a beautiful clarinet—from one king to another—and was obviously delighted with Benny's gift.

During the concert, some players managed to forget about their lost day because all the time we were on the stage four or five different Siamese waiters kept coming around with four or five different kinds of drinks. They'd put your choice of booze on a small table beside your music rack. No one drank much because you can't play Goodman charts in the bag, but we all agreed it was a nice welcoming gesture to the band!

I was hit by a car the first day I was in Bangkok. I didn't know they drove on the left side of the road there. I stepped off the curb, looked to my left, and saw that no cars were coming. I didn't know what hit me. A windshield of a car from my right smacked me in the shoulder and spun me around. The

Siamese driver looked terrified. No serious injury, but ever since then—November, 1956—when crossing a street I always look *both* ways.

I learned about open *klongs* (drainage canals) in Bangkok, too. These klongs are not to be confused with a toilet you can flush. When the wind is blowing your way from a klong, beware. Shortly after arriving in Bangkok, I noticed a curious smell and said to trumpet player Mel Davis, "Hey, I wonder what that funny smell is." Mel knew. "Man," he said, "that's canal number five."

The King of Thailand had a recording studio in his palace and did some recording with Benny, Budd Johnson, and the rhythm section—pianist Hank Jones, drummer Mousey Alexander, bass player Israel Crosby, and me—while we were in Bangkok. I'll never forget how the king arrived for this record date with Benny. He pulled up in front of the palace in a fancy Daimler and was dressed in white flannel slacks, white tennis shoes, and a white Siamese silk shirt. He played okay and claimed he couldn't get any better because he couldn't go out and sit in with other musicians because of protocol, because he was the king. He said he could only play with relatives and assorted royalty who were all very amateurish. But he did play with Benny Goodman and not many amateurs have done that! He played some standard tunes with Benny and, to my knowledge, the only copies of this kingly duet are to be found in the King of Thailand's recording studio. Anyhow, we all had a delightful lunch on one of the verandas with the king but—being king—he had to sit at a different table! (According to the Goodman discography by Russ Connor and Warren Hicks, *BG On the Record,* a tape of the king playing *On the Sunny Side of the Street* on soprano sax with the Goodman sextet was broadcast over the NBC radio network on January 1, 1957.)

Benny has made many recordings that were never issued for one reason or another. For example, he taped several of our concerts in Rangoon, Burma, during this tour, as the Connor and Hicks book points out. And I remember a marvelous arrangement of Cole Porter's *It's Bad for Me* for a 1955 Goodman sextet I recorded with in New York. Ruby Braff was on that date, played beautifully, and I thought it was an exceptional version of a great, tough tune. It was never released, although Benny later used the same arrangement on a recording date with Rosemary Clooney. Benny also had dozens of unissued tape recordings he made in concerts, nightclubs, rehearsal halls, and studios. I understand that all these tapes, according to his will, are now in the hands of the Yale Music Library. (In 1988, Yale began issuing a series of never-before-released Goodman recordings from this archive and its first LP includes another tune we did on that 1955 session. This was *Soft Lights and Sweet Music,* taken up, with fine solos by Benny, Braff, and Urbie Green. It's said to be pianist Dave McKenna's only record date with Benny.)

Our reception in Tokyo on that tour of the Orient was one that shocked Benny. The shock involved Jack Rains.

Rains had served in the Army in Japan and, at that time, had played in a Japanese band in Tokyo called The Blue Coats. I understand the band attempted to copy the Glenn Miller sound and the Glenn Miller look, complete with blue coats. When Jack heard that I was in the Goodman band rehearsing for the Far East tour, he told me he'd love to be in that band just to get back to Tokyo. And when he asked me if there was a chance to audition for Benny, I said sure, knowing Jack to be a fine player. "Just come on up," I told him. "I can't just go up and say Mr. Goodman, I'd like to audition," he said. "Of course you can," I said, "and I'll tell Benny you're coming up because the band isn't set yet."

So Jack came to the rehearsal and as he was warming up, Benny said, "Boy, he's got chops!" Benny hired him quickly that day.

Now, about that welcoming in Tokyo, 1956. There wasn't supposed to be a big reception for us at the airfield, but there was one. A mob of people was on the visitor's deck, and, as Benny walked out on the platform, all the people started to yell, "Jack Rains, Jack Rains, Jack Rains!" Benny said what the hell is this, knowing nothing about Jack's popularity as a member of the Japanese Blue Coats. "I was never so shocked in my life," Benny said later, laughing. When Benny got out of the way and Rains came off the plane, the cheers were overwhelming. The crowd obviously cared more about Jack Rains than it did about Benny Goodman. Rains must have been a big star in that Japanese band.

During the 1960s and 1970s, Jack was in the orchestra at Radio City Music Hall. A fine player, Jack Rains, and I'm glad I was able to help him make his triumphant return to Tokyo.

I will never forget another incident with that Goodman band. This took place at the beautiful long bar at the famous Raffles Hotel in Singapore. I had gone there with Budd Johnson, the band's excellent tenor saxophone player. Budd had been with the Earl Hines band for a dozen years and also with Count Basie and Dizzy Gillespie. All the people at the bar were brown-skinned Malaysians, well-dressed business types who looked as if they had plenty of money. It was cocktail hour and we stood at the bar with a woman on my left and a man next to her. I noticed the man kept trying to pull the woman away from me and toward himself. I had a fresh shave and was wearing a spanking clean seersucker suit.

I said to Budd, "Do I smell funny or something?"

Budd said "No," and with a smile added: "How do you like it?"

I didn't like it, suddenly realizing again how it is for blacks in the United States. In Singapore he was acceptable, I was not.

Yes, He Was Particular

Benny Goodman knew who he was. By 1937 he was one of America's most famous people and, as James T. Maher has written, "the most widely applauded instrumentalist—classical or popular—in American history." Though sometimes ill at ease outside of a musical environment, you never caught him saying any other jazz clarinet player was his match. And why should he? Benny was the best.

I remember when Budd Johnson first came into Benny's band and had just listened to Benny play *Poor Butterfly,* the lovely ballad Raymond Hubbell wrote in 1916. Benny loved to play this old tune and played it beautifully. As Benny finished, Budd turned to me on the bandstand and said, "That man's tone is so big it sounds like all four of us (sax players) when we play clarinets in unison."

After joining Benny for the first time, I soon discovered he was extremely particular about the way he wanted rhythm guitar played. In fact, he was particular about every instrument in the band.

Benny liked the rhythm guitar to be tight and crisp and light. Almost like a snare sound, so you can barely hear the notes. I had been praised for having a big walloping sound that cut through the twenty-two-piece Boyd Raeburn band, but I knew Benny didn't like it that way. He didn't want it the way Freddie Green played with Count Basie, either. He didn't want to hear the guitar as much as he wanted to hear a rhythm *section.* He wanted the bass, drums, and guitar to snap together, lightly and tightly. It will swing this way if you do it right.

Benny was known as a critic of drummers. He was also a critic of guitar players. I recall the first time I rehearsed *Sometimes I'm Happy,* as arranged by Fletcher Henderson years ago for Benny. I remembered the original record well, with Bunny Berigan on trumpet. It was a lovely chart, and I started to play so that the chord changes were distinct behind the sweetly singing saxes. Benny stopped the whole band.

"What the hell are you doing?" he asked me. "That's a *rhythm* instrument.

I don't want to hear each chord. The piano and horns will play the chords. You just play light, swinging rhythm." I said, "Well, I thought it sounded so pretty that way." He said, "Well, I don't want it that way." So he didn't get it that way.

But I had very little trouble working with Benny. He liked the way I played and I loved the way he played. And there was no cheating on chord changes with Benny, whether he wanted to *hear* each chord or not.

Benny could get upset at a rehearsal and blow his top occasionally, usually over someone playing too loudly or not phrasing as precisely as he wanted. But he would forget all about it the next day and be jolly. Johnny Frosk, a fine trumpet player who worked with both Benny and Tommy Dorsey, used to say that was the huge difference between the two leaders. Benny was not the type to hold a grudge, said Johnny, but Dorsey was and could be not only antagonistic but malicious. Jimmy Dorsey, on the other hand, was known to all sidemen as just about the kindest, nicest leader in the business. It's easy to understand why brothers Tommy and Jimmy fought so much. They were complete opposites, sweet and sour. To my knowledge, Glenn Miller was the only other big band leader disliked by his players as much as Tommy Dorsey was.

As for the famous "BG ray," said to be a devastating, withering stare that Benny used to reprimand musicians who did something that displeased him, I never got it and I never saw it. Maybe it was something Benny did in the 1930s and 1940s and he had mellowed by the time I worked with him in the 1950s. And Bobby Hackett once suggested that Benny's blank stare usually wasn't directed at a musician, but was simply Benny's way of concentrating on music, running through melodies in his head. In any event, during my four years with Benny I never saw him give anyone "the ray."

And I've heard many stories about how he couldn't, or wouldn't, remember names. Singer Helen Forrest, in her book, says that Benny called everybody "Pops," including her. So, he may have used "Pops" the way many musicians use "man," but he called me and many other musicians I know by name.

Benny's well-known quest for perfection was made clear to me when I watched him audition players for his band. One time he had a saxophone player auditioning and he told him, "Okay, you play the third alto part with the rhythm section only." That's a challenge. He expected the man to read the part perfectly and swing at the same time, with no melody, no lead alto to play with.

And at the Waldorf-Astoria one time he did something I have seen no other leader do. There was about two feet of space on each side around the bandstand, so this king had free rein and could walk around and watch what everyone was doing if he wanted. One night he wanted to do just that. Rex Peer was in this band playing second trombone (Urbie Green played first trombone) and the band was playing *Big John Special*, as I recall. Benny walked around the side of the bandstand, faced Rex and played the second trombone part right along with him! Then he walked back to the reed section, faced third alto player Al Block and played his part along with Al. The band got a kick out of that. I guess Benny played those old arrangements like *Big John Special* so many times he knew every part. But it was still a tour de force of musicianship and I wondered how many people in the room, jazz experts included, appreciated what he was doing.

At one band rehearsal, Benny called to say his car had broken down on the Merritt Parkway coming from Connecticut. He said to tell our lead trumpet player, Jimmy Maxwell, to go ahead and rehearse three new arrangements and he'd be there as soon as possible. And so we did. We worked especially hard with one new chart and thought it sounded great. So Benny finally arrived and we went through the arrangement. Benny said, "That sounds good, but . . . " He changed this, changed that, took out mutes for a certain section of the piece, and then we played it again. It sounded like a different band! It was infinitely better Benny's way. I said to Jimmy Maxwell, "Well, what do you think of that?" He said, "Well, I guess that's why he's down there in front and we're sitting back here!"

Benny could be curiously terse. One day in Las Vegas I went to have lunch at a restaurant next door to the Last Frontier Hotel and Benny was sitting there reading a newspaper and having dessert. "Hey, come on over and sit down," he said. I did and he kept reading his newspaper. I ordered a sandwich. Finally he looked up and said, "I notice most of the big bands aren't using guitar players any more." What did this mean, I wondered, is he going to get rid of his guitar player, me? I said, "Yes, but the hip ones have guitar players. Count Basie, Les Brown, and you." And he said, "Yeah," and went back to reading his paper. End of conversation. That's Benny. I was a bit shaken.

Benny was particular about tempos. Maybe it's because he came of age when dancing was so closely tied up with jazz. John Hammond said Benny loved to dance, and Hammond's wife, Esmé, said that Benny was a great dancer. If this is true (I never saw him dance), it might relate to his inordinate concern about tempos. I do know he ran tempos over in his head before kicking off a tune. He did this for a minute or even longer sometimes. And he even did it when his band was on the air, creating "dead air" for broadcast engineers and driving them up the wall. But Benny didn't give a damn, he wanted the right tempo and I guess he tried slightly different tempos for a tune over in his mind. In fact, Benny sometimes sang a tune to himself to help determine the tempo. He once said, "If you can't sing a song at a fast tempo, then it shouldn't be played at a fast tempo." And when he did, finally, decide on the tempo, he would say "al-so" (al as in Al, not as in also). With Benny it was "al-so, 1-2, 1-2-3-4." I didn't know what "al-so" meant when I worked with Benny, but someone told me recently that *also* is a German word, maybe Yiddish too, meaning "thus" or "like this." So now, at long last, I understand why saying "also" before counting off the tempo makes sense. But Benny is the only leader I ever worked with who used the word for this purpose. Maybe some symphony conductors use it, I don't know.

Benny was particular about nearly everything to do with music. My first recording date with Jo Jones, the wonderful drummer who was with the first and best Count Basie band, is a case in point. This was a Goodman sextet date in 1954. When Jo set up, he didn't have a bass drum. Jo simply took his traps case and attached a pedal to it, and that gave him something similar to the sound of a bass drum.

Benny told Jo he wanted a bass drum, but Jo said, "No, man, I always make albums this way."

Benny said, "But not with me."

He told Jo he'd have to have a bass drum and that was it, period.

Benny had someone go to Manny's music store to rent a bass drum, and while we waited for the bass drum to arrive we rehearsed without Jo. Benny didn't want him playing brushes without that bass drum, even in rehearsal. Jo was displeased but it was Benny's band and his recording date and he never hesitated to call the shots. As Bud Freeman has said, when it came to getting music the way he wanted it, Benny was a tough guy.

On this date I was playing a crisp, tight style that Benny wanted as usual when Benny said "cut" because he wanted to talk to the engineer. Jo said to me, "Man, don't play so damn tight, let 'em roll out, let 'em roll out."

"He doesn't want it that way," I said.

"I don't care what he wants, you let 'em *roll* out because that's the way it's supposed to be," Jo said.

Jo wanted me to play every chord deeply and clearly, to play like Freddie Green, I guess, but I told him I'd better keep it tight because "this is Benny Goodman's band and he wants me to do it that way."

So Jo was mad at me. But his anger didn't last long. And for the record, I think Jo Jones was one of the greatest small jazz band or big band drummers in the history of the world.

Benny liked a light sound from his saxophones, too. When recording he was often in front of the baritone sax player mumbling "quiet, quiet, quiet" or hushing him down by hand and mouth signals.

Benny was always strong for careful, long rehearsals. Practice was the name of the game for him. On a 1979 TV show, Frank Sinatra said he had tried to model his own work on Benny's approach to practice, explaining that he once asked Benny why he was constantly doodling backstage with his clarinet, and Benny replied, "That's so that when I'm not great, I'm good."

Pianist John Bunch, frequently in Goodman bands, had it right when he said, "Most people practice because they have to, but Benny practices because he loves it."

And as quoted by pianist Marian McPartland in her 1964 *Down Beat* piece on Goodman, I understand Bunch when he added this: "He'll rehearse for hours, and we'll all be getting tired, but he'll just be ready to play! One night he came down to the Half Note and sat in with Al Cohn and Zoot Sims, and he cooked everybody right off the stand. He must have taken ten and fifteen choruses on every tune. We're all a bit younger than he is, but we were exhausted when he got through, and there he was, fresh as a daisy, and ready to play some more!"

To my mind, Benny was, well, Benny. A self-made man, always his own man, and, unlike some musicians who reached celebrity status, never a show-biz type currying favor with anyone, but always the proud musician. As a young man attempting to lead a pit orchestra, long before any band was called a swing band, it was understandable that Benny failed as a pit band leader because, as he said, "I thought *they* [the dancers on stage] were supposed to follow *us!*"

As Bobby Hackett said, Benny was something like an absentminded professor when he was involved with music, finding it difficult to think of anything but music no matter what was happening. For example, Zoot Sims told me about a strange "encore" Zoot had during Benny's tour of Russia in 1962. Zoot had finished a solo to thunderous applause. And Benny said to him, "Play an encore. What do you want to play?" Zoot named a tune and Benny said, "Gee, I haven't played that in a long time" and kicked it off. This was with just the rhythm section. "Benny played three choruses and out," Zoot said, "and I stood there like a damn fool with the saxophone around my neck. He played *my encore!*"

Benny could go out of his way to help another musician. Alto saxophonist Walt Levinsky, who is also a terrific clarinetist, was glad to be working with a Goodman band but was terrified of flying. I noticed on one of our flights that his knuckles would get white from clutching the arm rests, and he couldn't eat. He wouldn't even have a drink until we landed. He finally told Benny that he simply couldn't continue because of all the flying. Benny said okay, I understand, and immediately called some studio people he knew in New York and told them that he would highly recommend Walt for any first chair saxophone job in any staff band. So Walt left the band, went back to New York by train and entered studio work.

Levinsky, incidentally, asked me a curious question between Goodman sets one night. "You're the chord master, do you think Benny can really hear all those changes?" He was serious.

"Gee, that's a silly question," I told him. "Yeah, I think he hears all those changes. Listen to him." Benny was playing on the changes better than anyone else could, including Walt Levinsky, including anyone. It's still a silly question.

And it was Levinsky who delivered one of my favorite lines about Benny. It was about 7 A.M. and we were gathering in front of a hotel to take our bus to the airport. Benny wasn't there. Suddenly we heard the sound of a clarinet from one of the hotel rooms. "My God, is that Benny practicing at this time of the morning?" I said to Walt. "Sure, that's Benny," he replied. "He's half man and half clarinet."

Levinsky played the Artie Shaw clarinet parts on the Time-Life album of old Shaw arrangements. Goodman was asked about a similar set. Benny said, "No, I'm still playing." Shaw stopped playing clarinet many years ago. And in 1987 and 1988 Levinsky led the fourteen-piece "Great American Swing Band" in New York that celebrated the Goodman charts and other famous big band arrangements and featured former Basie star Frank Wess as well as former Goodman sidemen Urbie Green and Warren Vaché.

Arthur Rollini, brother of the more famous Adrian Rollini (who played bass sax with Red Nichols, Joe Venuti, and Bix Beiderbecke in the 1920s, then became a popular vibes player in the 1930s), told me a memorable Benny story. I worked with Art in the Bradley band and he had played tenor sax in Benny's band from its beginning in 1934 until 1939. As Arthur tells it, one night in 1938 at the Madhattan Room in the Hotel Pennsylvania in New York, Benny kept changing clarinet reeds and started to put the unsatisfactory reeds in the piano. After a few nights, he had quite a pile of reeds there. And after depositing still another reed in the piano, Benny said to Arthur, who doubled on clarinet as did the other sax players for some arrangements, "Gee, your clarinet sounds good, let me try that reed you have." Benny liked Arthur's reed. "How come I can't ever find one so good?

You don't mind if I use it, do you? Take one out of the piano," he told Arthur, "it will be good enough for your section work." Arthur said okay, knowing that the reed Benny liked so much Benny had put in the piano earlier that night.

So, most all clarinet players, not just Benny, are always screwing around with reeds. For one guy's taste, there are only about four good reeds in a box of twenty-five.

Benny was known for saying curious things. And rightfully so. He said curious things. I'll never forget a brief conversation I had with him about Tommy Dorsey, shortly after Tommy died. This was in 1956 and we were in Rangoon. Some USIA people had invited a few members of the band to join them one afternoon at the British swimming club. Benny was there, too, and during conversation with me, somehow Tommy Dorsey was mentioned. Benny said, "Yeah, it makes me feel strange. Those things happen in threes." (This was a few months before Jimmy Dorsey died, but no other prominent swing band leader became number three at that time.) Thinking of Tommy's reputation as a tough man to get along with, one known for temper tantrums, I asked Benny, "What was Tommy Dorsey really like?"

His answer astounded me. All he said was "I don't know. I never met the man." End of conversation.

He *must* have met the man. Benny made a good many recordings with Tommy in the early 1930s, before either had a band, and had a few all-star record dates with him when both were famous. I seem to recall pictures of them together, too. I think Benny's answer to my question was just his way of sidestepping the question. That's how Benny was.

It should not be forgotten that Benny was the first white bandleader to feature black musicians. John Hammond, a wealthy man (his mother was a Vanderbilt) and relentless fighter against racism, no doubt encouraged Benny to do this in 1935, but Benny is the one who did it. And as Teddy Wilson, the first black with Benny, has said, Goodman had to argue continually for Wilson's and Lionel Hampton's sleeping accommodations and use of hotel restaurants, "*North* and South." With Wilson and Hampton, Goodman led the way in breaking down racial barriers in music and show business, and this was a dozen years before Branch Rickey broke the color line in baseball with Jackie Robinson.

Dozens of black musicians have been in big and small Goodman bands. Dozens of Italians, Jews, WASPs, and a few Hispanics, too. A man's musicianship was always what counted with Benny. Other prominent bandleaders of the late 1930s, such as Jimmy Dorsey, admired Benny for hiring blacks but said they could not do so and survive on the road. What with his great commercial and artistic success, Benny could say, as he told an Atlanta hotel owner who informed him he could not play in Atlanta if Negroes were in his band, "If you want me, you get them." (They got them.) It was no surprise when Benny invited top musicians from the Count Basie and Duke Ellington bands to join him on stage for his famous 1938 Carnegie Hall concert.

Of all the comments about Benny's playing, one of the wisest was by Bob Wilber, a fine clarinetist who played tenor sax in a 1958 Goodman band. In his 1988 autobiography *Music Was Not Enough,* Wilber said this: "Benny Goodman was the greatest natural clarinet player who ever lived. He heard a sound on the clarinet that nobody else heard in any kind of music, and he had a concept of the instrument that was so musical, like a singer's voice. He played with incredible ease on an instrument that is extremely difficult to play in a free relaxed way, but it was done so effortlessly that he made it seem like the easiest thing in the world." And there was "never a feeling of technique for technique's sake. Everything was purposeful, and at its best it had that marvelous rhythmic drive and hotness. Neither was there any hint of sentimentality when he played pretty tunes." Wilber said Benny developed a way of "treating a melody with such restraint that he literally forced the listener to say, 'Gee, what a beautiful song.'" Which reminds me of what Benny once gave as his reason for saying Ella Fitzgerald was his favorite singer: "She sings like I play."

Although I hadn't seen Benny for many years when his wife Alice, John Hammond's sister, died in early 1978, I sent him a short note. It read, simply, "Dear Benny: It's a sad old world. Take good care of yourself. Sincerely, Steve Jordan." I soon received a nice, handwritten, proper note of thanks from the Goodman family.

I saw him later that year in Washington at the National Press Club, where I played with a local jazz group the night Benny's sextet was the big attraction. He seemed glad to see me and enjoyed recalling the Far East trip. He asked me to get out my guitar and play a few chords. He had always liked the sound of my old unamplified Gibson. As I played, he said, "That guitar sounds better than my guy's!" By "my guy" he meant Cal Collins, the fine electric guitar player with his group. Later, Cal was warming up on his guitar and Benny said to me, "Hey, you know what? His guitar sounds better than yours!" Typical Benny. You never knew what he might say from one moment to the next. That was the last time I saw him.

And several years later when I was recovering from my bout with throat cancer, Benny got my home number somehow (from a mutual friend or the union, probably) and called to wish me well. I recognized his unmistakable voice as soon as he said "Ste-ee-ee-eve." I wondered if our old friend Helen Ward had put him up to it, but he insisted he had heard about my problem "through the grapevine." He asked if I needed any money. That was real nice of him. I thanked him and said no. He said if the situation should change, just to call him. I suggested he ought to get thirteen or fourteen pieces together again, with me on guitar of course, hit the road and show them all how it really should be done. Benny laughed, saying he didn't think he had the stamina for that and was exhausted after two concerts in one night at Carnegie Hall. We chatted about the old days. That's the last time I talked to him.

Benny died of a massive cerebral hemmorrhage at the age of seventy-seven on June 13, 1986. On the previous Saturday, June 7, he played his last gig at Wolf Trap Park near Washington, D.C., fronting a band of young men in a concert dedicated to the memory of Fletcher Henderson. A friend of mine who was there up front said that, although Benny was obviously in some physical pain, whether from his old sciatica problem or his heart (he had a pacemaker and had recovered from a serious aneurism and a lengthy operation in 1983), Benny was in a jolly mood, having fun playing the old Henderson charts he loved and jamming on *Poor Butterfly* and *Lady, Be Good*. And his singer, Carrie Smith, perhaps knowing that all was not well with Benny, cried as Benny played his closing theme, *Goodbye*. Benny had told a *Washington Post* reporter two months earlier, "If I'm going to go, I'm going to go playing." And he did. He had other performances scheduled at the time of his death.

It was a pleasure for me to have swung so many nights with the King of Swing. Benny Goodmans don't happen in music, or in any other art, very often.

4

MEMORABLE RECORDING DATES

I'll never forget a March 12, 1955, recording session at the Columbia Studios on 30th Street. The studio had been a church and the acoustics were extremely good. The producer of the date was Irving Townsend. I felt complimented to be the only white musician in a band that included trumpet player Buck Clayton, drummer Jo Jones, tenor saxophonist Budd Johnson, and the famous "Hawk," Coleman Hawkins, the granddaddy of jazz on the tenor saxophone.

I'll never forget this date because it was the day after Charlie Parker died. We didn't know of his death until Hawkins arrived. "You won't believe this," he said, "but Charlie Parker died last night." We were stunned. Almost in unison, we all said, "what?" Then Jo Jones said softly, and, for me, unforgettably: "The Hawk said the Bird is dead."

Parker, a great innovative alto saxophonist who was the hero of the bop generation, was only thirty-four when he died, but he looked much older because of heavy drinking and serious heroin addiction.

At this session, one without written music of any kind, I noticed, during playback of one of the tunes, how Jo Jones was listening, with drumsticks in action and his foot on the drum pedal, playing precisely everything he had played on the recording. Quite unusual. Buck Clayton told me, "Jo could always do that."

I've played on hundreds of recordings, (fifty-two sides with the Bradley-McKinley band from 1939–41 was only the beginning) and it's difficult for me to remember just when I recorded what with whom. But *B. G. in Hi-Fi*, a Capitol LP recorded at the Riverside Studios in November, 1954, was a memorable date because this was a great band and the recorded sound was exceptional for those days. I also played in the sextet with Jo Jones, Mel Powell, Charlie Shavers, and George Duvivier. With trumpet solos by Ruby Braff, the band brought new life to Benny's old charts. The trombone section was Will Bradley, Vernon Brown, and Cutty Cutshall, and you won't find a trio of trombone players like that on many recordings.

I made a number of sessions produced by John Hammond for Vanguard, a small company noted for producing the best recorded sound in the business as well as for producing previously unrecorded Bach (this was done in Europe with several different symphony orchestras). One of the Hammond dates was the 1953 *Mel Powell Septet* ten-inch Vanguard LP. The tunes are *'S Wonderful, It's Been So Long,* introduced by Benny Goodman with vocal by Helen Ward in 1935, *You're Lucky To Me,* and *I Must Have That Man,* which Billie Holiday sang so well. About the last one, John Hammond wrote: "For seven minutes and three slow choruses there is an intensity of feeling shared by all of the soloists that is almost unprecedented in popular music." I think John may have been overstating it, but he was enthusiastic by nature. I suggested *You're Lucky To Me,* a Eubie Blake song seldom played. Everyone knew it and everyone wanted to play it. We took it up. It swung. Henderson Chambers, not as widely known as the others at that session and who was about to join Count Basie's band then, certainly played some great trombone on that one.

On all the tunes, Buck Clayton's crackling trumpet and Ed Hall's clarinet playing sound as exciting today as they did that day in December, over thirty-five years ago. It's easy to understand why Goodman, not quick to praise other clarinet players, was quick to praise Ed Hall. So it was mutual. Although he certainly didn't sound like Benny, Goodman was Hall's favorite clarinetist, a fact that may surprise some who mistakenly believed Hall, perhaps because he used the older Albert system clarinet, to be a traditional player, not a swing player.

And Mel Powell plays beautifully. I can't remember any time I worked with Mel when he did not play beautifully, no matter what the tune or the tempo. I guess he *always* plays beautifully. We also had quite a rhythm section that day, with bass player Walter Page and drummer Jimmy Crawford, who was with Jimmie Lunceford's great band for more than a dozen years. Mel also played one solo, a serious composition of his own, *Sonatina for Piano.*

The *Buck Meets Ruby* session for Vanguard in 1954 was an exciting one, too. As the title suggests, Buck Clayton and Ruby Braff, then a twenty-seven-year-old newcomer to big-time jazz, shared trumpet honors. Trombonist

Benny Morton and tenor saxophonist Buddy Tate, both, like Buck, formerly with Basie, helped to keep things cooking. Sir Charles Thompson, who wrote *Robbins Nest*, a big hit for Illinois Jacquet, was also on this date. And immediately after our sterling group completed a great walloping final chorus for one of the tunes, Sir Charles said: "Well, I wonder what all the jazz critics who can't play anything will think of that!"

I also enjoyed being on all three of the Vic Dickenson Septet LPs for Vanguard. Braff and Ed Hall were on these, too. With or without plunger mute, Dickenson talked on the trombone and his accent was his own.

And when I think of Vic, my mind takes me to a surprise birthday party that John Hammond's wife, Esmé, decided to give John at their summer place in Westport, Connecticut. I'm sure it was no surprise to John. There were too many people involved. Esmé hired the musicians individually, musicians she knew John liked, including Ruby Braff, Ed Hall, me, and Vic Dickenson. This shindig was held in a barn, and Ed Hall and his wife pulled up in a beautiful, chocolate-colored Jaguar. He was wearing a homburg hat and looked like some kind of dignitary. Esmé greeted everyone warmly with a kiss on the cheek and a hug. There were three bartenders and it was a real millionaire's party. Vic came in with George Avakian and Vic looked like he was suffering. "Oh, I'm so delighted to see you, Vic, it's so nice of you to come," said Esmé, "and now," she added, pointing to the bar, "what would you like?" Vic's one-word reply sounded like a dying man's last wish: "*Juice!*" he said, loudly with feeling.

(Esmé was John Hammond's second wife. They were married in 1949. A onetime debutante of the year and former daughter-in-law of RCA board chairman David Sarnoff, Esmé produced the Eddie Condon jazz show during the early days of TV and certainly shared John's enthusiasm for jazz. In June, 1986, I called John following the death of his brother-in-law, Benny Goodman. "Yes, too bad about Benny," he said, and added, to my sorrow and amazement, "It's been a sad time. I buried my wife two weeks ago." Esmé, a lovely woman, was sixty-six when she died. The cause of death was pneumonia brought on by a 1981 blood transfusion containing an AIDS virus. John—who did so much to help so many jazz musicians, including Benny, Count Basie, Teddy Wilson, Billie Holiday, Lester Young, and Charlie Christian—suffered a stroke in June, 1985, and died at seventy-six in July, 1987. John was a tireless fighter for racial equality and good music.)

A 1954 recording for Columbia, made in Carnegie Hall, had me teaming with two true giants in the rhythm department, bass player Milt Hinton and drummer Jo Jones. This was *Mel Powell and His All Stars*. Other players were Braff, Clayton, Tate, trombonist Urbie Green, and clarinetist Tony Scott.

I recorded with Coleman Hawkins again on another Vanguard session produced by John Hammond (*Sir Charles Thompson Band*). I was the only white musician on this 1955 date. The other musicians were Thompson (piano), Emmett Berry (trumpet), Benny Morton (trombone), Earl Warren (alto sax), Aaron Bell (bass), and Bobby Donaldson (drums), Fats Waller's cousin. Berry, Morton, and Warren were Basie band veterans. Berry, too often overlooked in jazz history books, was a standout with the bands of Fletcher Henderson, Horace Henderson (a better pianist than his older and more famous brother Fletcher according to Hammond, and his arrangements swung more than Fletcher's, according to Clayton), Teddy Wilson, Lionel Hampton, Benny Carter, and John Kirby even before he joined Basie!

And in 1956 or 1957, I was part of a superb big band playing great Nelson Riddle arrangements based on Army bugle calls. Riddle had been a sergeant during World War II and was familiar with many of the calls. The album was designed to cash in on the popularity of "Sgt. Bilko" as played by Phil Silvers on TV. The Columbia LP was entitled *Phil Silvers and His Swinging Brass*. But because Nelson Riddle was under contract to Capitol Records, his credit line on the album cover is small and reads "Compositions Conceived by Nelson Riddle." Note that "conceived," as if Riddle only chose the bugle calls, sketched out a few ideas, and didn't write the arrangements. Indeed, in the liner notes, two other arrangers are credited for arranging the music. I'm sure Riddle did most all of the writing. But contracts are contracts.

And there's an interesting story behind the band we had on this date. Irving Townsend, the album's producer, told me that Nelson Riddle had told him that the album would have to be done in California because he couldn't get a band good enough in New York! Townsend was astounded by such a thought. He told Riddle, "Whaddya mean we can't get good enough musicians in New York?" Perhaps Riddle had been in that California sun too long. In any event, Townsend informed Riddle that they would do the album in New York with New York musicians, period!

And Townsend certainly did come up with a remarkable band, as Riddle soon discovered when he came to New York for the date. Riddle was obviously delighted with the work of the musicians during this recording session, as anyone would be, and when the album came out I noted that liner-note writer Townsend made sure everyone knew these were New York musicians. "This great band," he wrote, "was carefully chosen in New York."

Here's that band. Trumpets: Bernie Glow, Jimmy Maxwell, Charlie Shavers, and Dale McMickle. Trombones: Will Bradley (not listed on the album for some reason), Urbie Green, and Jack Satterfield. Saxes: Hymie Schertzer, Sid

Cooper, Al Klink, and Boomie Richman. Clarinet: Artie Baker. Drums: Don Lamond. Bongos, chimes, vibes: Terry Snyder. Guitar: Me. Piano: Hank Jones. Bass: Frank Carroll. (Carroll and Snyder, not as well known as most of the others, were both on NBC staff for many years.)

Hymie Schertzer's singing alto is featured on the lovely *Two Arms* (based on the bugle call "To Arms") along with great obbligato playing dubbed in after the recording by Urbie Green and Boomie Richman, who used earphones to do this. There are many fine clarinet solos by Artie Baker, too, and the knowing ear will hear the Artie Shaw influence in his work. It's amazing how those few notes in the dozen bugle calls could be developed so ingeniously by Riddle.

A Ruby Braff quartet set for Epic in 1956 (*Braff!*) is well recorded, with the guitar up front. On one of the tunes, *It's Been So Long,* it's just Ruby and me on the first chorus. Ruby was in great form throughout this date, as was our pianist, Cape Cod's Dave McKenna, a devout Boston Red Sox fan. Dave, who had big band experience with Woody Herman and small band education with Charlie Ventura and Bobby Hackett, is more widely known now than he was in 1956. Since then, he's been profiled in the *New Yorker,* has been seen on TV with singers Tony Bennett and Rosemary Clooney, and has a large body of fans who cheer his solo piano at Boston's Copley Plaza, where he has had steady gigs in recent years.

Another album I made with Ruby features tunes associated with Bunny Berigan, the great trumpet player who drank too much and was dead at thirty-three in 1942 (*Hi-Fi Salute to Bunny* on RCA Victor). Inimitable clarinetist Pee Wee Russell is on this date, and once again I had the pleasure of working beside Walter Page on bass. Yes, Ruby plays *I Can't Get Started* with proper Berigan warmth and gusto.

In 1957 I was on what was billed as "Jimmy Dorsey's last recording" and I'm still nonplussed about it. I had recently returned to New York from Benny Goodman's Far East tour and had left Benny in March that year. I got a call one evening for a record session to be held at Webster Hall, an old East Side ballroom on 11th Street near First Avenue. The session was to begin at 10 A.M. There was no mention that it was to involve Jimmy Dorsey's orchestra, which had been billed as "The Fabulous Dorseys" until Tommy died in October, 1956. Jimmy died in June, 1957. At the time of Jimmy's death, the band had no guitar player, but they wanted one for this recording and I was chosen. Perhaps they tried and for some reason could not get Sam Herman, a fine player who had been the band's last guitarist.

I was appalled when I discovered that morning that the music was to be passed off as Jimmy Dorsey's last recording session. Jimmy Dorsey was already buried. I was introduced to Jimmy's twenty-two-year-old daughter, a sweet and pretty girl, and then to Dick Stabile, who had been flown in from Los Angeles to imitate Jimmy on alto saxophone and cheat people into believing that this was, indeed, Jimmy's last date.

Stabile did a wonderful job, although he was reminded a few times that he hit squeak notes that Jimmy never did. Several times the engineer yelled things like "Dick, lay off that F over F!" At one time, Stabile was famous for his high-register skill, and even while imitating J. D., which he did very well, vibrato and all, through force of habit he couldn't help but squeak some exceptionally high notes now and then.

One of the takes was *So Rare,* which had been a hit for Jimmy in 1936, and with this recording it became a big hit all over again. You will still find it in some juke boxes. But it's a fraud. It isn't Jimmy Dorsey's orchestra and it's not Jimmy on alto. It's a fine band, with studio players such as Will Bradley, combined with some who had worked in Jimmy's last band, notably Johnny Frosk and Dick Perry, but the record is a lie.

I hope that Jimmy's pretty daughter received some of the thousands and thousands of dollars this one take of *So Rare* made. With all due respect to Dick Stabile, I still wonder how he could have participated in such shysterism.

So, Stabile made many bucks out of it, as did the record company (Fraternity) and the juke box people. Why couldn't they have tried honesty, instead, and simply called it Jimmy Dorsey's orchestra featuring Dick Stabile? Stabile—who was then no longer a big name—became "Jimmy Dorsey" and did a good job of imitation. A *good* job. But Jimmy Dorsey was a *great* player, not merely a good one. Jimmy was also one of the kindest of big band leaders, quite unlike his brother. For this reason, I'm not sure how Jimmy might react to "his" last recording, but if brother Tommy could come back I'm sure he'd throw hand grenades at those who dreamed up this money-making scheme and got away with it. And I'd be the first to applaud such meritorious action.

I notice that Leonard Feather's *Encyclopedia of Jazz* says, "Ironically, a single record that Jimmy Dorsey made some months before his death for the Fraternity label, *So Rare* . . . was his first hit in several years." It gives me pleasure to correct that common mistake. Believe me, Leonard, Jimmy Dorsey was in his grave when that recording was made.

And *So Rare* was not the only take "Jimmy Dorsey" recorded that day that brought money to cheaters. Two pieces designed as "big band rock" did fairly well, too.

Morning sessions can be troublesome for some musicians, particularly those who worked late the night before, then had a few drinks and little, if any, sleep. I well remember one 9 A.M. recording date about 1958 that included two great trumpet players, Billy Butterfield and Charlie Shavers. Both had been tasting the night before. Charlie had been playing at the Metropole until 3 A.M. and Billy had worked late, too. Each told me he had had about three hours of sleep. They were plainly hung over and tired, though cleanly shaven and neatly dressed.

We began by running over an arrangement for "notes." No one blew very hard, because for notes you are simply looking for copyist errors. If you find one, the arranger checks his score and tells you what the notes should be. I was seated next to the trumpets and, as the band ran through the arrangement for notes, I heard Billy tell Charlie that he didn't feel too good and hoped he could last out the date.

Charlie replied: "Butterball, I got a double trumpet case and only one trumpet." He opened it and the one supposedly vacant side was lined with half-pint bottles of applejack. Both Shavers and Butterfield promptly had a few swigs of that applejack and were able to last out the date. Indeed, both played beautifully, cutting everything with grace and ease, maintaining their reputations as masters of the trumpet. Charlie's applejack supply apparently saved the day for both of them.

In 1958, I cut an LP with Cootie Williams, the famous Duke Ellington star, and one of Benny Goodman's favorite trumpet players, too. This was an RCA album called *The Legend of Bessie Smith* and featured Ronnie Gilbert singing songs Bessie did. She didn't remind anyone of Bessie Smith, but this was quite an all-star band. In addition to Cootie, there was trombonist Benny Morton, clarinetist Buster Bailey, pianist Claude Hopkins, bassist George Duvivier (another Goodman favorite), and drummer Osie Johnson.

It was during this session that Claude Hopkins, who led a popular big band during the 1930s, and wrote the hit tune *I Would Do Anything For You,* told me he invested his money years ago, bought some tenement houses, and became a "slum lord." I said, "Well, okay, Claude, if you say so. But give them some heat and hot water." I guess real estate does pay off better than music.

I made the only LP album under my own name in 1972: *Here Comes Mr. Jordan, The Great Unplugged Guitar* (Fat Cat Jazz Records). I understand it was sold a few years ago to the Jazzology label. The only other musician on the date is bass player Billy Goodall, who worked in Tommy Dorsey and Charlie Barnet bands. There are twenty-one songs with fifteen vocals by me. My composition, *Steve's Waltz,* is included.

The 1973 Chiaroscuro album *Buddy Tate and His Buddies* was recorded on a Sunday because of me. Producer Hank O'Neal called to say that Buddy Tate wanted me for the date with Roy Eldridge, Illinois Jacquet, Mary Lou Williams, Milt Hinton, and Gus Johnson. But the only night off I had from a regular gig in Washington was Sunday, and I told him it would be tough for me to take it and, anyway, there were a lot of good guitar players in New York. "No, no, Buddy wants you, not anybody else," O'Neal told me. So, the date was scheduled for a Sunday, and six prominent jazz musicians had to rearrange their schedules to fit mine. That was nice of them and good for my ego. That's also the reason why the old standard, *Sunday,* is on the album. After we had finished recording the special tunes for the date, a new piece by Buck Clayton, two by Buddy, and one by Mary Lou, we had time for one more. I suggested *Sunday* simply because it was Sunday and because I knew it was a tune all these jazz veterans knew and would be comfortable with. Or so I thought. Mary Lou, a veteran of countless jam sessions and one of the best pianists of the swing era, insisted she didn't know *Sunday.* I couldn't believe it. Nor could Roy. "*Everybody* knows *Sunday,*" Roy kept telling her, "Mary Lou, I know you know *Sunday!*" But she said she didn't, and when we decided to go ahead with it I wrote out the chord changes for her. And if you listen closely to the lengthy solo by Mary Lou on this recording I think you will notice that she doesn't play the melody of the song. I guess she really didn't know it. But it's a marvelous solo, anyway, as her solos always were, and conceived only from the chord changes, a kind of conception all good jazz players are able to achieve.

Buddy—a quiet, gentle, nice guy—was pleased with the set and I was glad he liked the rhythm section after making the date Sunday because of me. He described our rhythm section as "fat" and "nothin' but prime meat." Well, there can be no time problem working with rhythm masters like Mary Lou, Gus Johnson, and Milt Hinton. And it's always fun to work with Milt, not only because he is such a superb bass player but because he's always fun, always smiling.

I hadn't seen Illinois Jacquet for years, and he not only played as well as ever, he looked as if he hadn't aged at all. And let me add that anyone who thinks Illinois is not a great tenor saxophone player, merely a sensational one, doesn't know what he's talking about. Illinois can *play.* Some who know him only for those high-note, honking things he did for *Jazz at the Phil-harmonic* recordings and the Lionel Hampton band don't know enough about Illinois Jacquet. He's one of the best and always has been. Even today, he's still demonstrating what a swinging tenor saxophone really sounds like.

5

AT NO. 1, BLUES ALLEY

From 1965 until 1972, I worked regularly as part of the house band at Blues Alley in Washington's Georgetown, the oldest part of the city. In fact, Georgetown was a city long before Washington existed. Clarinetist and vibes player Tommy Gwaltney, a Virginian whose relatives created the famous Gwaltney ham and bacon business, built the club so that the trio and quartet he headed, including me, would have a steady place to play, to avoid hassles with clubowners and "so that people could listen to what we are trying to do." The former Bobby Hackett sideman soon discovered there were problems galore being a clubowner, but my years at Blues Alley were fun, mainly, because of the music.

In late 1964, Tommy bought an old building in an alley near the center of Georgetown, off Wisconsin Avenue and a half-block from M Street. It was just another old semihistoric building, believed to have been a stable for an undertaker's horses around 1800. The rebuilding job meant tearing down the front brick wall, but each eighteenth-century brick was retained and used in the reconstruction. We opened in January, 1965. Tommy named the place Blues Alley and gave it an address: No. 1, Blues Alley.

Tommy sold his two-thirds interest in the club in 1971. It has had several owners since, and, though the place sometimes still has good music, it is now, as Tommy says, "more like a dinner theater, not a club, with audiences being moved in and out after shows. All it has in common with the original club is the name and the location." Also, Blues Alley is mighty expensive today.

And a few words right now about a house band colleague at Blues Alley, a steady, sober, soft-spoken, modest man who is a great bass player.

For twenty years, from age twenty on, I was lucky to play with some of the finest bass players in the history of jazz. To name some: Felix Giobbe, Doc Goldberg, Eddie Safranski, Israel Crosby, Walter Page, Oscar Pettiford, Bob Haggart, Aaron Bell, George Duvivier, Irv Manning, Milt Hinton. When it came to artistry on the bass, I thought I had heard it all.

Then, in 1959, when I first came to Washington, I went to hear finger-style guitarist Charlie Byrd's trio and had another revelation about bass playing: Keter Betts. I had never heard of this Washingtonian before and I'll never forget that first night I heard Keter. He was just great! Fine tone, great ear, keen selection of cleanly played notes, amazing speed, ingenious solos.

About six years later he joined the Gwaltney Quintet at Blues Alley and I worked with him there for four years. He left Blues Alley to go on the road with Ella Fitzgerald and he stayed with Ella for nineteen years. Even now, if Ella decides to do a gig, Keter is her first-call bass player. In my opinion, Keter, teamed with guitarist Joe Pass, gave the great Ella what is probably the greatest support she ever had.

During my seven years at Blues Alley, there was much swinging music. Tommy brought in famous players from New York and elsewhere to play with our group, including Bud Freeman, Roy Eldridge, Pee Wee Russell, Teddy Wilson, Zoot Sims, Lou McGarity, Charlie Shavers, Bobby Hackett, Peanuts Hucko, and many others equally prominent. Lots of good singers, too. Even a great tap dancer, Baby Lawrence.

Assorted Blues Alley memories follow.

While having a drink between sets with Al Hibbler, the blind singer who was with Duke Ellington's band for eight years, I asked him how he managed to get around New York. "How in the world do you do it? Do you have a Seeing Eye dog?"

Al's answer was quick. "Oh, no, man," he said, "I have a seeing eye woman!"

Clark Terry is a great guy as well as a great trumpet player. When he arrived at Blues Alley to play a two-week engagement, he discovered that the rest of the band—our small house band led by Tommy Gwaltney—would be in tuxedos. Clark said he had three tuxes at home but hadn't brought one from New York. He asked me where he could buy one in a hurry. I told him there was no need to do that because he was the star of the show and didn't have to dress like the band. But he would have none of that and immediately went to a nearby Georgetown shop and found only expensive tuxes. He kept looking and finally found a schlock shop somewhere. He knew he was in the right place when the owner said, "Hev I got a tuxedo for you?" The tux cost only $39.95 ("I pay that much for my shirts," Clark said, laughing) and it fit fine, with cuffs the only alteration. But don't get the idea that Clark was cheap. After we closed on the last night of his two-week gig, he threw a food and booze party in his Georgetown suite for everyone who worked in the club—waitresses, bartenders, everybody. It was quite a party and it might have cost him a whole week's pay.

I watched Teddy Wilson come into Blues Alley on a cold winter night, blow on his hands once and, without a piano warmup of any kind, kick off an up-tempo tune and play with machine gun rapidity as cleanly as possible with *both hands*. Teddy sat up straight on the piano bench like a music professor and talked something like an English professor. He chose his words as carefully as he chose his chords. His piano playing was precise and elegant, and when he had a point to make he could be just as precise and elegant in his speech. His father headed the English department at Tuskegee, where his mother also taught, and if Teddy hadn't become a musician perhaps he might have been an English teacher like his parents.

When I was on the Goodman-Armstrong tour in 1953, the contrast in personality between the two famous pianists with us—Wilson with Goodman and Joey Bushkin with Armstrong—was striking. We used two buses, but Armstrong sidemen would be in our bus sometimes. Teddy would be reading *Harper's* or the *New Yorker*, or Tolstoy, maybe, while Joey, a wit and a clown, would be urging the bus driver, doing about twenty in town, to drive faster. "Hey, Bart," he yelled to the driver one day, "pull over, there's an old lady in a wheelchair trying to pass us!"

Teddy spoke softly. Even when he was drinking, which was seldom, he never raised his voice. When he was at Blues Alley I used to drive him to his hotel and he continually urged me to come in for just one drink. It was usually more than one and sometimes it was five o'clock in the morning by the time I left. One night the room clerk called up, angrily complaining about the loud talk. It must have been me or the other guest, former Columbia Records engineer Bill Savory. It couldn't have been soft-spoken Teddy. But Teddy got on the phone and told the clerk that he must explain to those complaining that "I'm a night person. I live at night, and that's why I'm here with my friends living at night." And the clerk is telling him that *they* live during the day and *they* have to sleep and get up in the morning to go to work and we must try to keep it down. And we did. When Teddy was at Blues Alley he said he would frequently sleep until six in the afternoon, have some breakfast, and then come to work.

The late Bobby Hackett, a superb cornet player and one of the nicest people ever in the music business, or any other business for that matter, told me the following story between sets at Blues Alley one night.

When Bobby was working with singer Tony Bennett in a Pittsburgh hotel, two guys in what Bobby called "the horse-racing business" told Tony they had a singer they wanted him to hear. He was a big, handsome, athletic blond guy, they said, and they thought he was quite a singer, too, but they needed an expert's opinion. "We've already spent $10,000 on his arrangements, clothes, and promotion," Tony was told, and if Tony could possibly come over after he'd finished his show and listen to the young singer's final set at a nearby club they'd be most grateful. They wanted Tony's frank opinion. So Tony went to hear the singer and Bobby went along, too.

After the youngster's performance, Tony told the two horse-racing businessmen that, in his opinion, the young man didn't have much of a voice, sang out of meter, and that what was wrong with his singing could not be corrected by teaching. "And it's just too bad that you've spent all that money on him," added Tony.

At hearing this, one of the guys immediately said to the other one, "Okay, so we'll make him a fighter."

The late Clancy Hayes was one of the best singers I ever heard. He made his first trip to Washington in 1967 to work at Blues Alley. When Tommy introduced him, he said: "Clancy Hayes comes direct from the San Francisco club, Earthquake McGoon's." Clancy grinned and said: "That's no club, that's a saloon!" Well, Clancy should know. He was working in Oklahoma oil field honkytonks when he was fourteen. He left the road in 1926 to settle in San Francisco and remained there except for occasional tours with Bob Scobey's band during the 1950s.

In 1967, Clancy was fifty-nine but looked older. He was bald, walked as if he had a back problem, and was having trouble with his eyes. He was on a job with Benny Goodman once and said that it amused him that Benny kept calling him "Mr. Hayes." He was quick to point out that he was only a few months older than Benny.

But though he may have looked older than he was, when he sang in his clear, crisp voice, the years faded away and he sounded much younger than his age.

Clancy was known as a banjo player but he didn't play banjo, he played guitar. More precisely, banjo guitar. His axe was a banjo but it had six guitar strings on it and he played guitar chords.

Clancy was a walking encyclopedia of old songs. He seemed to know them all, verses included. I've never heard anyone sing *I Ain't Gonna Give Nobody None of My Jellyroll, Hindustan, Silver Dollar, Ace in the Hole, Rose of Washington Square, Oh! By Jingo,* or *Down in Jungletown* the way he did. His phrasing was marvelous. They said he was irreplaceable when he was alive and they were right.

Another singer I had never heard in person until she came to Blues Alley was Lurlean Hunter. What a voice! She sang a slow ballad without fuss or strain and she sizzled on up-tempo tunes. She also articulated each word, so listeners could get those lyrics right.

Lurlean is not as well known as she ought to be, and this is because she has always preferred family life in Chicago to the road. She confined most of her nightclub work to Chicago. As she told me, on the road she "misses the children."

At Blues Alley, she liked to do some songs with just guitar accompaniment. One of these was *My Ship,* and when we did this one, the audience was speechless, entranced.

Tony Bennett dropped into Blues Alley one night after working a big-paying gig elsewhere in Washington. I don't know how much money he was paid for his singing earlier that night, but I know he sang only for kicks with our band. And as always, he sounded great.

Tony loves jazz, which is why he has hired great players like Bobby Hackett and Ruby Braff to work with him and why Ralph Sharon is his regular pianist. I notice that Tony keeps grumbling about the lack of attention now given jazz and great composers like Irving Berlin. A March, 1988, Associated Press interview had him saying, "In Japan, they have more jazz clubs in Tokyo than in all the United States." A frightening thought, but maybe he's right. And I give Tony credit for resisting record company attempts to "update" his sound, to get away from his jazz feeling. He says he was without a major-label contract for fourteen years because he refused to relinquish control of how his songs are presented. He recorded on small labels with Zoot Sims and Bill Evans instead.

Sol Yaged, the clarinet player who is always trying to play like Benny

Goodman, is a funny guy. As we left the bandstand at Blues Alley one night, Sol said, "Gee, you sound great, Steve," and in the same breath, "How do I sound?"

At Blues Alley, Sol was a true pied piper. When the crowd was sparse one evening, he said he'd have to do something about that. So he went out on the street in Georgetown, playing his clarinet, to drum up trade. He came back to the club about twenty minutes later, still playing the clarinet, with half a dozen new customers behind him.

Roland Hanna, a marvelous piano player who toured Europe with·Goodman in 1958 and worked with the late Charles Mingus, too, was featured at Blues Alley when a popular Washington pianist in the Cy Walter tradition, Mel Clement, came in after hours and began to play. When he finished, Hanna, impressed, went over to Mel and said softly: "I saw your hands and I heard your mind." Hanna is a tiny guy, like Milt Buckner, and when he plays piano he sits on telephone books.

When it comes to music, there is no substitute for practice, study, and self-criticism. One of Washington's best pianists, John Eaton, is a case in point. When I worked with him in the Tommy Gwaltney Trio in the early 1960s, and this was before Tommy built Blues Alley, John was a young man trying to learn his trade. He was somewhat stiff on occasion, but his playing seemed to improve all the time. He worked at it. Although he concentrated on solo work elsewhere, he rejoined the Gwaltney group at Blues Alley on occasion. John is now doing what few pianists are able to do: Play solo jazz piano on fine pianos in the best rooms and solo concerts for the Smithsonian Institution.

A Yale graduate who majored in English, not music, John was an unusual product of his bop generation. He was much more interested in the music of James P. Johnson (how many players his age then had even heard of *Carolina Shout?*), Fats Waller, and Willie (the Lion) Smith than in Bud Powell and his emulators. While working jazz jobs at night, for many years John continued serious formal study with New York's Alexander Lipsky, who had no interest in jazz at all. Lipsky flew down to Washington each week to give lessons to John and several other students.

E. Howard Hunt is a friend of mine. Music brought us together. I got to know him when he was still with the CIA, before he retired and moved to the White House and into that Watergate mess.

He introduced himself to me at Blues Alley because he liked the way I played guitar. I was soon to discover that he had been a member of the original Modernaires—organized at Brown University during the 1930s—and might have stayed with that soon-to-be famous singing group, but after graduating from Brown decided to continue his education at the Sorbonne in Paris. I can tell you that he sings any harmony part extremely well. As he says, he "has a knack for it." He played trumpet in a college band and plays what you could call arranger's piano. One night when Tony Tamburello and his wife were visiting my wife and me, the four of us were at Hunt's home one evening, and while Tony played the piano, Howard got out his trumpet. "I've got no chops at all," he said, "but I can make eight bars or so on some simple tune." And what he played wasn't bad jazz.

Before he took the job at the White House, he used to say that he was going to retire soon. He'd have more time for writing—he had written twenty-eight books, mostly paperback spy novels—and more time for music, too. After his move to the White House, Blues Alley opened for lunch and the only live entertainment at lunch was me, singing old tunes and playing solo guitar. He would bring his colleagues from the White House in for lunch and he insists that I've met and talked with Gordon Liddy, but I don't remember doing so.

Before his wife died in that Chicago plane crash and after the Watergate burglary was page one news, I asked him how in the world he ever got mixed up in such an ungodly mess. He said he was just "an office boy" and that he was happy that they couldn't take his CIA pension away. He said he could rely on that because it was only a breaking and entering charge, not a crime against the federal government. He was, of course, to discover differently. While others involved with Watergate got off scot-free, he was given seven years. It seemed unfair to me at the time and still does. Seven years for burglary? He wound up spending thirty-three months in prison, then was paroled.

Howard said his office was a tiny cubicle at the White House. No filing cabinets. He filed his papers on the floor. He also told me that when he tried to see Charlie Colson during his first day there he had to go through fourteen aides, and he found Colson to be snobbish and unhelpful. John Dean also gave him the cold shoulder. Howard said all he did was follow Colson's orders. He said Colson set the whole thing up.

As few people know, Howard got into spy work only because of an injury suffered while he was in the Navy. When the war broke out he was in Paris at the Sorbonne. He had to get out fast, so he and some student friends worked their way back to the States on a Swedish freighter. Then he joined the Navy and was injured in a storm on the North Sea. After recuperating, he couldn't meet Naval physical standards so he received a medical discharge. He could not have been drafted and many in his circumstance would have said "I've done my part" and taken a job on the home front. Not Howard. He found a way to get into the OSS, where he learned to fly. On his last OSS mission, he was in a plane over central China, parachuting bundles of supplies to a radio group reporting on Japanese army activities. The OSS became the CIA and he stayed aboard for many years. Then, much to his future sorrow, he moved into Nixon's White House.

He once thought that Nixon "personified all that was best in America and his enemies were my enemies," but he thinks differently today. According to a May, 1979, interview in *People* magazine, Howard believes that Nixon knew in advance of the first Watergate break-in and ordered the second. He also thinks that Nixon erased the famous eighteen-and-a-half minutes on the White House tape made three days after the second burglary.

The last time I talked to Howard he said that no publisher seemed to be interested in his book about his jail experience. "They all say the book is too depressing," he told me. Is a book about jail conditions supposed to be comic?

In early 1978, at the age of fifty-eight, he married Laura, who had been his daughter's Spanish teacher. They lived in Miami but recently moved to Guadalajara, Mexico. Howard says he can live there for what his air conditioning cost in Miami. I hope he finally has time for his writing and music listening. Howard Hunt is a nice guy who got swindled by a bad crowd.

One time Tommy Gwaltney needed a kidney stone operation and decided to have a surgeon he knew in his hometown, Norfolk, do the job. So he went there for the operation and had to leave the hospital, not without pain, in a wheelchair. Butch Hall, an optometrist and a good guitar player, too, came with Tommy's wife, Betty, to pick him up and wheel him away. They used Butch's car and Tommy noticed Butch had his guitar case on the floor of the car. Tommy wondered if Butch might be intending to play guitar for him to cheer him up after they got to Tommy's house. Tommy wasn't in the mood for that but didn't want to say anything to put Butch down because Butch was such a nice guy. Sure enough, after they got Tommy home, Butch came into his bedroom with his guitar case. Oh Lord, Tommy thought. But when Butch opened the guitar case, there was no guitar. It was full of fried chicken. So they had fried chicken. Butch had never let on. That was Butch's style.

Many singers sing the wrong words to certain standards. And this was true of two of the great singers we featured at Blues Alley.

Jimmy Rushing, the inimitable "Mister Five-by-Five," continually fouled up *I'm Gonna Sit Right Down and Write Myself a Letter,* the Fred Ahlert–Joe Young song that Fats Waller made famous. Jimmy used to sing: "I'm gonna write words, oh, so sweet, they're gonna knock *you* off your feet, a lot of kisses on the bottom, *you'll* be glad you got 'em . . ." That's not right. You are writing a letter to yourself. The words are "gonna knock *me* off my feet." As for those kisses on the bottom, "*I'll* be glad I got 'em."

And few noticed when cute little Maxine Sullivan sang "when Edison *discovered* sound" in George and Ira Gershwin's *They All Laughed.* Edison didn't discover sound. He *recorded* it.

We had just finished a set at Blues Alley with a rip-roaring Dixieland standard. I think it was *Muskrat Ramble.* Or maybe *Shim-Me-Sha-Wabble.* One of those ancient swingers. It might have been too hot for some of the "cool" jazz fans in the club, but Tommy told the audience: "Man, if you don't like that, you don't like fried chicken. And if you don't like fried chicken, you don't like America!"

SIX GREAT TRUMPET PLAYERS

Buck Clayton

I loved Buck Clayton. He was a great musician and a delightful guy.

In recent years he'd had more than his share of bad luck. In 1969, he had a precancerous lesion inside his lip, not uncommon for trumpet players. Louis Armstrong had the same problem, had lip surgery, and couldn't play for a year. Then shortly after Buck began to practice his horn again, he lifted a rock in his back yard and wound up with a double hernia. He couldn't play for a long time after that because when you blow a trumpet you can easily split the stitches.

Though still getting some royalties from his records, he was working at the musician's union in New York to make ends meet, and when his hernia healed sufficiently he practiced trumpet again and starting building some chops. But soon thereafter, while on tour in Switzerland, he discovered he had a deviated septum that needed emergency treatment. Then a dental bridge problem cut his lips up so much when he tried to play that thirty stitches were required. Also about this time, while he was walking along Madison Avenue, a motorcycle hit a car, jumped over the curb onto the sidewalk, and the handlebar of the motorcycle hit Buck and broke his left wrist. That meant he couldn't even hold his trumpet.

All that was about a dozen years ago. Buck almost gave up. And soon after he started playing again he was on the critical list for two weeks at Jamaica Hospital with a bleeding gastric ulcer. Following an operation, while heavily sedated in the hospital, the nurse had the radio on softly in his room, and Maria Muldaur was singing "come on, come on, come on." Drugged and half asleep, Buck told me, "I remember thinking it was Billie Holiday up there telling me *come on,* Buck, *come on,* and I wanted to go!"

Somehow Buck weathered all these mishaps, and although he finally had to give up trumpet playing, he's remained in music as an arranger.

In 1977, while planning a tour of Africa for the State Department, he came to Washington to meet with State Department people about the tour. He stayed at my home while in town, and one night we invited Wally and Chris Garner to join us for dinner. Wally Garner is one of the best clarinet players in Washington and the Garners are friends of Buck. Buck had been drinking vodka all evening and when the vodka bottle was dead he switched to Scotch. When dinner time came, Buck wasn't hungry and only wanted to sip his Scotch. Long after the Garners had left for home, my wife Patty finally talked Buck into having some dinner. This was about 2:30 in the morning. When he got up the next day, he asked Patty: "Did I eat anything last night?" Patty said: "Oh, yes, you had roast beef, potatoes, salad, and broccoli." Softly and with a smile, Buck replied: "That's nice, I like broccoli!" Patty broke up.

Buck told me the following story about himself. He calls it "my most embarrassing moment."

He had finished work at 3 A.M. at the Metropole in New York and on the way to the subway station realized that he needed a men's room. He also realized that the men's rooms in the subway were locked between midnight at 6 A.M. because of muggers and homosexuals.

Knowing he'd never make it home without bladder relief, he spotted an empty alley, and had no sooner started his essential task when a voice said, "Okay, let's see your identification. When you get through, of course." Buck says this policeman must have come out of thin air.

Buck showed his credentials and tried to explain his predicament. The policeman told him he could "explain it to the judge Tuesday at 10 A.M.," and handed him a ticket.

The most embarrassing moment came in court when Buck found the judge to be a woman and he had to explain it to her. He said she wasn't embarrassed at all, but he was. All she said was, "Pay the bailiff $15, next case."

An amazing guy, Buck Clayton. Everyone interested in jazz remembers his work with the original and best of all Basie bands. Jazz enthusiasts also rightfully cherish his many recordings under his own name and with Teddy Wilson, Billie Holiday, and Benny Goodman. And some are aware that he has written arrangements for Basie, Goodman, and Ellington. But how many know that in 1934, a few years before he joined Basie, he led a thirteen-piece jazz band in Shanghai? He spent almost two years in Shanghai and speaks several Chinese dialects.

When he was staying with the Jordans in Alexandria, he found he couldn't make the 8 A.M. Metroliner train to New York. My daughter Julie called to see if his reservation could be shifted to the 12:30 Metroliner. Once the operator heard the name, she asked, "Is that *the* Buck Clayton?" "Yes it is," said Julie, "He's right here, would you like to talk to him?" "Wow, would I!" she replied happily.

Informed that the operator would like to talk to the famous Buck Clayton, Buck stood up, forgot his hangover, smiled, looked nine feet tall, picked up the phone and said, sweetly, "Hello, baby, this is Buck Clayton."

He got the reservation he wanted, and maybe he made that operator's day.

Charlie Shavers

Charlie Shavers was a jolly, outgoing guy who laughed real hard when he heard something funny. He was also the kind of person who could go to sleep for three or four minutes and appear completely rested. And he was an absolutely marvelous trumpet player. I always enjoyed working with Charlie.

Although inspired by Armstrong, Shavers was no imitator of the world's best known and most admired jazz musician. Shavers always had his own thing going. His playing was distinctive, to put it mildly. A Shavers solo on any recording was always easy for anyone familiar with jazz trumpet styles to identify. Shavers always played Shavers.

He had exceptional technique, a brilliant tone, great range, and the ease with which Charlie could play difficult passages cleanly at extremely fast tempos often seemed incredible. I remember when I was rehearsing with a Benny Goodman sextet in 1954 when we ripped into *Air Mail Special* at the usual rapid tempo. It was the first time Charlie had played this with Benny, I think, and the clarinet champ was plainly amazed at the way Charlie could cut the tune with so much precision, almost as if he were fingering a piano lightly, not blowing a trumpet. Charlie played the tune in thirds with Benny and Mel Powell, a part originally designed for Charlie Christian's single-string guitar wizardry, not for a trumpet player. When we had finished *Air Mail Special,* Benny looked at me and said, "He does it with only three fingers, too."

Charlie could do anything on the trumpet and do it well. If labels are necessary, he was a swing musician I suppose, first gaining fame for his playing, composing, and arranging for John Kirby's light and breezy six-piece band in the 1930s. But he could play Dixieland, too, and he could play a slow ballad beautifully with impeccable taste. Indeed, he could play softly into a mute with such control that his trumpet sounded like a violin. And when sensation was needed, Charlie could be as sensational as anyone who ever put lip to horn. Loud. Soft. Open horn. Mute. Section work. Whatever. Charlie Shavers could do it all.

He had a lively sense of humor, too. In 1956, when he was working with the Tommy Dorsey band, after Jimmy Dorsey got together with his brother again and the band was therefore billed as "The Fabulous Dorseys," I happened to be having a drink with trombone player Al Lorraine at Kelly's bar across the street from the Statler (formerly Pennsylvania) Hotel where the Dorsey band was playing. A half-dozen of the Dorsey guys came walking in and they were all laughing and saying "s-s-s-sweetheart!" Every other word they said, to the bartender, or to themselves, was "s-s-s-s-sweetheart," like a hiss.

I asked one of them, trumpet player Dick Perry, what the hell all this s-s-s-sweetheart was about. Amidst laughter, he told me what happened.

The Dorsey band had just finished a coast-to-coast half-hour radio show. Just before the band went on the air the last tune was a slow pretty ballad. Charlie Shavers had a solo in the middle, using a tight mute, and was playing softly and prettily when he hit a clam. Tommy Dorsey immediately ran over to him with his fists clenched, yelling "I'm paying you all this money and people are dancing and you can't even play a goddamn solo right" or something like that. But Charlie kept on playing, right in his face. When the tune was finished, Tommy told the band to get ready for the radio show and he called out all the numbers they would be playing on the show. In a few minutes the band was on the air. Now remember, Tommy always started his theme song *I'm Getting Sentimental Over You* unaccompanied. The first line of the song is "Never thought I'd fall" and there is a small pause before the saxophone section comes in after the "fall" note. This time, Dorsey cracked on that note, fouled it all up. And during that pause before the saxophone section comes in, a voice from the band said "s-s-s-s-sweet-heart!" It was Charlie Shavers. Tommy Dorsey turned purple.

Dorsey was not popular with his players and they laughed about that s-s-s-sweetheart line between sets all night that night at Kelly's bar.

Charlie was involved in a tragic auto accident in Colorado in August, 1951, while on the road with Tommy Dorsey's band. Trumpet player Ray Wetzel, who handled the high notes for the Kenton band before joining Dorsey (when Kenton reorganized, seventeen-year-old Maynard Ferguson took over Wetzel's challenging high-note chair), was sleeping in the back seat of the car Charlie was driving. Ray's wife, Bonnie, a bass player, was in the front seat beside Charlie. A blown tire sent a speeding driver coming the other way directly into the path of Charlie's car. Charlie slammed on his brakes but hit him head-on. Wetzel was DOA at the hospital. His rib cage was crushed against the front seat and he had terrible internal injuries. His wife and Charlie went to the hospital with cuts and bruises but were not seriously injured. I should mention, too, that Bonnie Wetzel was one of the few female musicians good enough to work regularly with prominent jazz players, including Shavers and Roy Eldridge. She followed John Frigo as one-third of the "Soft Winds" trio, the other two-thirds being Lou Carter and Herb Ellis, before Herb replaced Barney Kessel in the Oscar Peterson Trio. Very pretty girl, too. She died of cancer in 1965.

I happened to work with Charlie Shavers shortly before his death, at Blues Alley in Washington. The last tune he played that Saturday night—perhaps the last tune he played on earth—was *For All We Know*, a beautiful ballad Nat Cole used to sing so well. Just before it ended, he stopped playing, pointed to pianist John Eaton to pick up his solo, and said to the audience, softly and sweetly: "For all we know, we may never meet again . . . and folks, that's true, we *may* never meet again, but until we ever do, whenever that time may be, may the good Lord think kindly of you."

Then he went home to New York that Saturday night, and I'm told he tried to make a gig on Sunday but couldn't because his neck hurt him so badly. It was cancer. He went into the hospital on Monday and they gave him a laryngectomy and he knew he would never play trumpet again. I talked to his wife, Blanche, by phone when I heard about this and she was crying. I told her about a friend of mine in Washington who had that operation and told her he got along well and that Charlie would still be able to write music. It didn't help much and I knew it couldn't help much.

He died two days after the death of Louis Armstrong in July, 1971. The brief Associated Press story reporting Charlie's death at fifty-four said that his death wish was to have his trumpet buried with Louis.

What happened was this: He did not respond to treatment after his laryngectomy. Not being able to speak after he left the hospital, he wrote
messages on a pad to Blanche, saying he wanted a sandwich, or whatever.
And after he read in the newspaper that Louis was dead, he told Blanche
by pencil on that pad that he wanted his horn to be buried in Armstrong's
casket. Presumably, Charlie did not know at that time that he was going to
die, but he did know that he would never play trumpet again and Louis
Armstrong had always been his trumpet hero. Buck Clayton told me later
that after Charlie died, Blanche didn't even try to get his trumpet in Louis's
casket because, as she put it, "That horn is never going anywhere again
where I can't go."

After Charlie's death, I called Blanche, whom I had never met, to offer
condolences. She told me Charlie was quite comfortable to the end. He just
lay in bed, she said, listening to records with a quart of vodka on his night
table at all times.

Like everyone else who knew Charlie Shavers, I miss him.

Roy Eldridge

Roy Eldridge was born in 1911. But the last time I played
with him, when he was in his sixties, he could still hit high notes on the
button, hard, then tackle the lower register a split second later with the
same accuracy.

At one time or another, Roy played with just about everyone important
in jazz. Lord knows how many jam sessions he was in, how many sessions
his very presence in town inspired. He led his own bands, large and small.
He was a key sideman in the big bands of Fletcher Henderson, Horace
Henderson, Teddy Hill, Gene Krupa, and Artie Shaw. He was in dozens of
fine small groups, including one Benny Goodman took to Europe. He was
one of McKinney's Cotton Pickers. He even worked for Mal Hallett.

Because Louis Armstrong's playing influenced Eldridge and Eldridge's
playing influenced Dizzy Gillespie, Roy has been called the "major link"
between Armstrong and Gillespie. This is the kind of stuff you get from jazz
critics who habitually overlook swing era giants. Roy was too important a
jazz player to be described as a mere "link" between any two other players.
His playing had fire, excitement, gusto, and unquenchable boldness.

When he was at Blues Alley in 1966, I understood what he was saying
when he said: "Look, I'm making more money now than I ever have in my
life. But the music business isn't good. There are fewer and fewer places to

work. Too many good musicians are out of work. Remember Hilton Jefferson, the fine alto player? He's a bank guard now. And some of the places you have to work. Take the Embers in New York. When I signed the contract there, I didn't notice that the contract included words saying that I had to use a mute all the time. I'll never work there again. . . . Things are different now. When I was with Krupa we used to work 346 days a year. That's right, 346 days a year. And for good money. Some of the bands that keep working now, well I'd hate to tell you what they get paid some weeks just to keep the band working. Woody Herman knows. . . . "

Roy also complained, rightfully, about how he had to break up one of the best groups he ever had, in the mid-1950s, a small band including tenor saxophone giant Ben Webster, drummer Jo Jones, and pianist Ray Bryant. "It was a crime to break that group up," said Roy, "but the agency couldn't find any jobs for us. Can you imagine?"

Many have tried to play like Eldridge, but no one has succeeded. Dizzy Gillespie finally gave up trying to cut Roy at his own game (it was no contest) years ago and wisely went on to develop his own distinctive style of jazz trumpet, creating a new approach to improvisation with Charlie Parker.

They called Roy Eldridge "Little Jazz" and the nickname was appropriate. Roy was small of stature and he was jazz as much as any man ever was. He always played *hot*.

Billy Butterfield

Another great swing era veteran, Billy Butterfield, was one I worked with many times, in recording studios, at jazz concerts, and in nightclubs. Butterfield, or "Butterball" as he was often called because of his round face and overall chubbiness, always had a fat tone, great range, and a command of the instrument that could remind you of Louis Armstrong in his prime. Billy never doodled around on trumpet as some popular young contemporary players do. He wailed loud and clear. During the swing era, Billy was a standout with Bob Crosby, Artie Shaw, and Benny Goodman. And as swing era veterans may recall, while he was with Crosby in the late 1930s that band's expert bass player and arranger Bobby Haggart wrote a beautiful instrumental piece to feature Billy's great range and sterling tone. It was called *What's New?* Lyrics were soon added and that's right, Linda Ronstadt fans, what was originally a Butterfield solo tune became a hit all over again more than forty years later.

A Blues Alley Butterfield story: my wife Patty was in the bar area of Blues

Alley one night when we were about five minutes into our second set. She noticed Butterfield, our guest artist that week, leave. Knowing that he had been drinking much more than usual, and that bandleader Tommy Gwaltney was about to introduce him, Patty figured someone should talk to him. She found him wandering around in the alley in front of the club looking for a cab. Explaining who she was, Patty asked him where he was going. Billy told her he was going down to Granby Street (a street in Norfolk, Virginia, 200 miles away, where Billy lived). She suggested that he should wait until Tommy got off the stand—he was staying with Tommy while working at Blues Alley. He agreed. They returned to the club just as Tommy finished introducing "the great Billy Butterfield." Billy walked on stage and played beautifully.

Another Butterfield story. Newton Thomas is a wonderful jazz piano player whom I worked with in Tommy Gwaltney's group in Washington. Newton is in North Carolina somewhere now selling musical instruments. When we were working opposite Charlie Byrd in the Showboat Lounge in Washington about twenty-five years ago, trumpet player Al Hirt came in. He had recently become a star, playing *Flight of the Bumblebee* on Dixieland tunes. He's too cold to be a jazz player but he has lots of chops. When Newton came off the stand, Hirt said to him, "What's your name?" Newton told him. "I really enjoyed your playing," said Hirt. "Where are you from?" Newton told him he was from Richmond and said the last band he traveled with was Billy Butterfield's. "Oh," said Hirt, "Billy Butterfield. Nice little trumpet player." Newton said, "Yeah," thinking what a strange understatement. Hirt said, "The next time you talk to Billy tell him Jumbo said hello." Newton said he would do that and a few days later Billy called him about a gig. Newton said, "Incidentally, Jumbo says hello." Billy said, "Great! Who the hell is Jumbo?"

And in the late 1940s, when Ray McKinley fronted a seven-piece group for a month on a sustaining basis for NBC radio, a band that included Butterfield, Deane Kincaide, and Felix Giobbe, McKinley began to grumble about this and that, giving his expert colleagues a tough time. Billy said, "I think they shot the wrong McKinley!"

It was in November, 1987, when Johnson "Fat Cat" McRee told me that Billy was not feeling well and wouldn't be at Manassas, Virginia, for the jazz festival the last weekend of that month. Later I heard that he had inoperable throat cancer and had been taking radiation treatments.

I had throat cancer in 1982 and am now okay. I can even sing fairly well. But my cancer was operable.

I got Billy's phone number from Fat Cat and thought I could give him some encouragement. I spoke to him five times from January until early March. The radiation is devastating and makes swallowing terribly difficult. Still, it's the best treatment there is. I lost 31 pounds in four months, then the weight loss stopped. Billy lost 76 pounds in three months. Dottie, his wife, told me Billy was always 200 pounds but had gone down to 124 pounds. He died at his home in North Palm Beach, Florida, March 18, 1988. Another good friend gone.

As for me, I'm just glad to be still here, and I think my surgery was a great help.

Ruby Braff

Ruby Braff is certainly one of the best trumpet players I ever worked with. Some say he was born too late because he wasn't swept up with Dizzy Gillespie's style as were others his age. In fact, Ruby plays more like the great trumpet players of the swing era, men like Bunny Berigan.

Ruby is also quite a wit. I'm glad the recording of the Ruby Braff Octet (including me) at the Newport Jazz Festival in 1957 preserves his introduction of our set. Ruby, with his classic Boston accent, put down all the serious modern jazz people who don't think jazz is fun and had people laughing at the same time: "We're not going to play any psychological or psychotic music. No fugues, no nothing. Just jazz music. And whatever you do, please don't feel like we're playing a symphony. I hate to see everybody looking stiff and formal." Introducing our first tune, Duke Ellington's *It Don't Mean a Thing If It Ain't Got That Swing*, Ruby added, rightfully, "and naturally it doesn't."

Ruby also spoke for many of us when he answered a reporter's question about the popular music scene, meaning rock, in the 1960s: "It's not for people whose tastes are cultivated to lower themselves to the tastes of foolish children."

And Ruby's witty remarks often involve a wild exaggeration. One time when he was almost starving, he asked George Wein, the jazz promoter and sometime piano player, if he could borrow two or three hundred. George told Ruby that he caught him at a bad time. "Can you imagine that?" asked Ruby. "When George's grandmother died she left him enough money to support everybody in the entire world for twenty-five years and he's having a hard time!"

Wild Bill Davison

Wild Bill Davison, the Chicago cornet player who became an important member of the Eddie Condon gang in New York, was a nut on military medals, military uniforms, military swords, military guns. It took him five years, but he finally assembled a complete World War II German officer's uniform.

Wild Bill told me that during the 1930s he almost went to jail over a Confederate pistol. He had found it in an antique shop in Chicago where it had been lying around for Lord only knows how long. He was most excited to have it and in a Chicago taxicab he showed it to the driver. "Look at this great antique pistol I just bought," he said. "It's great. Look at the heft of this thing." The driver was suitably impressed until Wild Bill pointed it at the windshield and playfully squeezed the trigger. It fired. The bullet went through the windshield, barely missing the driver's head. The driver was terrified, and as he slammed on the brake people came running over, soon followed by the police.

As the cop asked Wild Bill if he had a permit for the gun, he uttered the familiar words "I didn't know it was loaded." He did have a receipt for the gun, and by explaining his amateur status as a collector of military gear, managed to avoid jail.

Wild Bill said, "Maybe it was a Confederate way of getting back at the damn Yankees. Maybe it was planted in that antique shop with a bullet in it for revenge."

Bill was eighty-three when he died in 1989, fifteen days after surgery for an aortal aneurism. Shortly before his operation he was playing in Japan and had planned to be working in Europe at the age of eighty-four. He never had any formal music lessons, but he had an iron lip and a great ear for harmony as well as melody.

A Wild Bill deathbed story: Tommy Saunders, a Detroit trumpet player and good friend of Bill's, got a call from Anne, Bill's wife, explaining that Bill was very sick in the hospital and would not be making some gig they were both to play. Tommy decided to fly to Los Angeles to see Bill. He discovered he had been in a coma for a long time. But he told me he got out his horn and played some soft blues and that Bill moved his eyelids. "Bill, can you hear me?" asked Tommy. Bill came to, and said, "Who's that?" The doctor said, "This is one therapy we never tried before on anybody." But Bill died later that day.

7

MORE UNFORGETTABLE COLLEAGUES

Oscar Pettiford was a great bass player with a fatal flaw: He drove automobiles too fast.

I'll never forget a drive on the Merritt Parkway with him in 1954 or 1955. We had worked a birthday party gig for Bobby Gefaell, a wealthy jazz enthusiast who lived in Bedford Village, New York, right next to Greenwich, Connecticut. Bobby, a paper mill heir, had been a drummer in college and loved our kind of music. Ruby Braff led this band at this outdoor party on Bobby's beautiful patio. Others in the group were pianist Nat Pierce, drummer Buzzy Drootin, Pettiford, and me. It was a group that could really cook and a good time was had by all.

As we were leaving, Bobby gave each of us a quart of Scotch or a quart of whatever we wanted. I took Scotch and so did Oscar. Oscar suggested we have a few drinks on the patio and then he'd drive me back to New York. Otherwise I would have gone with Ruby who had driven me to the party. So Oscar and I hung around a while, and neither of us were feeling much pain when we got in the car about two or three o'clock in the morning.

We took the Merritt Parkway, where the speed limit had been cut down to 35 miles an hour on orders of Governor Abe Ribicoff who said there were far too many accidents on the parkway. But speed limit signs didn't trouble Oscar Pettiford. Once on the parkway he got his old Kaiser-Fraser cooking along close to 100 miles an hour. And we soon heard what I had expected to hear, a police car siren. We slowed down and a big tall Connecticut state trooper was soon asking Oscar for his license and registration. He couldn't help but notice Oscar's bass fiddle in the back seat and when he looked at the registration, he said, "Oscar Pettiford. Are you really Oscar Pettiford? *The* Oscar Pettiford?"

"Yessir, I am," said Oscar.

"Gee, no kidding," said the cop. "I've been a fan of yours for years. My son is, too. When are you going back into Birdland?"

"I don't know," said Oscar, "we're working on a possible date there soon. It'll be in the papers."

"Gee, I'd like to have your autograph," said the cop, acting like a teenage movie fan.

"Steve," says Oscar, "open that glove compartment and you'll find some new 45s in there."

Oscar got the 45 rpm records, asked the cop his name and his son's name, too, and signed two record labels, suitably, one for the cop and one for his son.

"That's wonderful, thanks a lot," said the cop. He then advised Oscar to take it slower because the parkway is dangerous. "Be sure not to go too fast," he said. Oscar thanked him.

The cop got back in his car, made a U-turn, and went in the direction whence he had come. Oscar revved up the car, and within seconds we were zooming toward New York again with the speedometer pushing 100 miles an hour. It was a harrowing experience but most any ride with Oscar was. And there was no point in telling him to slow down. He paid no attention to such advice.

I was saddened but not shocked when I heard in 1958 that this happy warrior and great musician was in serious condition in a Vienna, Austria, hospital after a bad automobile accident. He recovered and was able to play again, but suffered from a number of serious internal injuries, and he was only thirty-eight years old when he died due to those injuries in 1960 in Copenhagen. His death reminded me of Boyd Raeburn, whose internal injuries from an auto accident similarly led eventually to his death.

Pettiford was part Indian—indeed, he was born on an Indian reservation in Okmulgee, Oklahoma—and was the greatest bass player of his time. Greater than Mingus, Safranski, anyone. He played ingenious pizzicato jazz solos on the cello, too. In the late 1940s there was no other bass player playing solos to match those by Oscar. Lord only knows how many of the best ones today were inspired by his work. And he worked with just about everybody. At twenty-one he was with Charlie Barnet's band. He was with a Roy Eldridge group at the Onyx on 52d Street when it was "swing alley" and, with Dizzy Gillespie, was coleader of the first bebop group to work the street. He was featured with Coleman Hawkins, led his own groups, worked briefly with Boyd Raeburn's 1945 band, and was with Duke Ellington for several years. He was with Woody Herman's band, too. Oscar recorded with dozens of others—Miles Davis, Clark Terry, Sonny Rollins, Sonny Stitt, Lee Konitz, Thelonious Monk, Art Blakey, Jimmy Cleveland, Teddy Charles, Stan Getz, Eddie Heywood, Kenny Dorham, Urbie Green, many more—and could play any kind of jazz extremely well. Oscar also did some composing. Remember *Swingin' Till the Girls Come Home?* Or *Tricrotism?*

I spent a good many evenings with Oscar at Charlie's Tavern, a musicians' hangout in the old Roseland building that is no more. In the 1950s, if you wanted to find jazz colleagues you'd find them at Charlie's Tavern, Joe Harbor's Spotlight Cafe, or Junior's Bar, all in the same neighborhood. One night Oscar and I were leaving Charlie's about two o'clock in the morning. I lived on the East Side, on 53d between Second and Third avenues, and I was going to walk home. But as a big Greyhound bus came down the street, I said to Oscar, kiddingly, "I think I'll hail this cab and go home." I was carrying my guitar case.

To our surprise, the bus stopped, and pulled over to us. The door opened and Dizzy Gillespie was standing there, grinning broadly. "Hey Petticoat! Steve! What are you two doing?"

"I though you were a cab, ha ha," I said.

"Get in," said Dizzy, "and I'll take you wherever you're going."

Dizzy was going to South Carolina and he had a big band in that bus, fifteen or sixteen musicians plus a girl singer.

But Dizzy wasn't kidding. He said, "Driver, drop this cat off on the way to the Holland Tunnel." So I gave directions and he took me right to my door. He went about ten blocks out of his way to do so. Nice guy and dear friend, Dizzy Gillespie.

When I was discovering jazz as a teenager, Walter Page was the bass player on all those thirty-five-cent Decca records by Count Basie I cherished. He was one-fourth of what was called by some, with good reason, "the All-American rhythm section," namely Basie, guitarist Freddie Green, drummer Jo Jones, and Page.

I worked with Page in nightclubs and also in the Ruby Braff Octet that played at the Newport Jazz Festival in 1957, a swinging group that included Pee Wee Russell. As noted earlier, I also made a good many recordings with Page, several of these with his Basie rhythm chum, Jo Jones. Walter and Jo were always trying to put one another on, and Jo was always intimating that Walter was much older than he was. One day I asked Jo when he first met Walter and Jo said, "Oh, man, it was in Oklahoma City and I was just a little boy and my mother was holding my hand crossing the street and Walter was on the corner playing his bass with two mandolin players. That's when I met him."

Walter and I were working at the Village Vanguard for two weeks in 1957 with Ruby Braff, and at the bar between sets one night he kept insisting he was only forty-two years old. We knew damn well that was wrong. Later that evening after a few more tastes, he all but gave his age away when he said, "You know that lick Ruby was playing on that last tune? Well, that ain't new and Ruby knows it. And it's not as new as Ruby thinks it is, either. Ruby probably heard somebody play it in the thirties. Well, in 1916 I heard it on a gig in New Orleans." And he kept talking on and on about that gig. "Wow," I said, "you're forty-two years old and you're talking about a gig in 1916!"

And it must have been 1957 when I played a jazz concert in Greenwich, Connecticut, with a group led by Buck Clayton. It was an early affair and we had all been invited to a few hours of fun at Irving Townsend's home later.

It was there that Walter Page, after a few cocktails, divulged his priceless explanation of what jazz is all about. Asked by a layman to define jazz, Walter said, "Ya know Beethoven, Brahms and all those guys? Well, we just picked up where they left off!"

I wonder if the gentleman ever repeated Walter's novel explanation of jazz. He didn't look as if he would. He smiled, said thanks to Walter, and went back to the bar. Probably for a double.

Walter Page was a delightful man and a marvelous, marvelous bass player. He was a big man and his tone on that bass fiddle was as big as his size. Impeccable time, too.

Walter died at Bellevue Hospital in 1957, not too long after our discussion about his age. The obits said he was born in 1900, making him fifty-seven.

I called his wife when I heard he was sick. She said she had come home from work and knew something was wrong when she saw his bass fiddle laying downstairs at the bottom of the steps. They lived in a walkup and Walter would never leave his instrument for two minutes in a place like that. She found him on the sofa, looking terrible. She called a doctor right away and they put him in Bellevue. I went to see him at Bellevue with Bob Gefaell, but Walter was asleep all the time we were there. Walter's wife was there, too, and when the doctor came in I told him that if Walter needs blood, I've got Type O and can give it to anybody. The doctor told me that he would not need any blood because "the entire Count Basie band has been here and they all gave." I thought that was extremely nice, because half of the guys in the Basie band didn't even know him. But they knew who he was, I'm sure, and how much he had done in the 1930s to help make the Basie band so great.

Walter Page: Superior musician and lovely guy.

In Washington, I often worked with Tee Carson, for a long time one of the city's best piano players as well as a U.S. marshal. Because of his government job, he seldom played outside of the nation's capital, although he was on the road one time with Ella Fitzgerald. And in 1984, after Count Basie's death and after Tee had left marshaling, Tee became the piano player in the Count Basie band.

Tee told me in the early 1950s Art Tatum and Oscar Peterson were in Washington at the same time. Both had Sunday off and Tee invited them both to his home for Sunday dinner. Tatum told Tee that he had heard about Peterson but didn't know too much about him. This was shortly after Peterson had come to the States from Canada.

After dinner, both Tee and Peterson asked Tatum to play something, but Tatum begged off because of the big dinner. "I don't feel like playing," he said, before asking Peterson to play something. Peterson, in awe of Tatum, as most every jazz piano player in the world was, seemed reluctant but Tee and Tatum insisted, so Oscar played. Tee said Oscar's playing was marvelous. He seemed to be playing for his life. When he finished with an incredibly fast tempo, cut beautifully, he was perspiring freely. Tatum said, "That's kind of inspiring. I think I'll play something, after all."

Tee said that within a minute or so Tatum had done just about everything Oscar had done on the piano and much more. Oscar said to Tee, "Well, I guess I'd better give up piano." Tee said he has never heard Peterson play any better but Tatum was infinitely superior.

So, perhaps the death of Tatum in 1956 helped to establish Peterson, a lovely guy and certainly a wonderful piano player, though no match for Tatum.

Tatum was a genius and one of the explanations of the word genius is this: A genius can do readily what no one else can do at all. I remember talking about the meaning of the word at a party one time and I suggested that Thomas Edison was a genius. Oh, no, someone said, Edison was a mechanic, not a genius. He had the advantage of glass, he knew what tungsten was, and electricity was available. A genius, I was told, would have invented glass and discovered tungsten and electricity. A genius would have done the whole thing by himself. At the piano, Art Tatum had such genius. He could do what no one else could do or even dreamed of doing.

Jimmy McPartland told me everybody thinks he's playing Bix Beiderbecke's cornet. Jimmy said he's not. He explained it to me this way. "It's a cornet that Bix picked out but I bought it. He and I were in the music store together and he said, 'This is a good one here.' I tried it, liked it, and bought it. But everybody keeps telling me, 'Jimmy, we know that is Bix's cornet!'"

Jimmy took over Bix's cornet chair with the Wolverines in the mid-1920s. He had been a member of the Austin High gang in Chicago, a band that included Frank Teschemacher and Bud Freeman. In the late 1920s, he was with Ben Pollack's band along with Jack Teagarden and Benny Goodman. During World War II, he took part in the Normandy invasion as a Ranger and earned five battle stars. In Europe he met English pianist Marian Page, who became the famous Marian McPartland. They were married in 1945, divorced in 1970 but continued to play gigs together, and remarried two weeks before his death in 1991. Jimmy was a real nice guy.

As mentioned earlier, in 1957 Ruby Braff organized a small group, including me, to play at the Newport Jazz Festival. Ruby had rented a nice house in a Bronx suburb and thought it would be a good idea to have us come over and run through some of the tunes we'd play at Newport so we'd sound like a band and not like a half-dozen guys at a jam session. The last guy to arrive was the inimitable Pee Wee Russell. And he had quite an explanation for being late.

"I would have been here sooner but I had trouble on the subway on the way up here. My clarinet case was on the seat beside me and a dirty-looking guy came over and started to pick it up. I said, 'Don't touch that clarinet case' but he started to open one of the latches."

Then Pee Wee drew himself up to his full 5' 9", 120-pound stature and said, "Now, I'm no Rocky Marciano, you know," a remark indisputable and one that made us laugh, "but I hit him good and he ran into the next car. Nobody fools with *my* clarinet! At the station I had to sit on the bench for a while to calm down. That's why I'm late."

No one in the world ever played the clarinet, or any instrument for that matter, with more conviction, more heart. Pee Wee always came to play. You never knew just what he might play on the next chorus because Pee Wee didn't know either.

Pee Wee once said, "I never consciously sought a dirty tone for affect and I never considered myself a Dixieland clarinet player." That Pee Wee played much jazz that was not associated with Dixieland bands was a fact that more and more people finally began to realize. But the idea that Pee Wee's playing changed, that it became more "modern," is nonsense.

As Coleman Hawkins said after making a recording with Pee Wee Russell about twenty-five years ago: "For thirty years I've been listening to him play those funny notes. He used to think they were wrong, but they weren't. He's always been 'way out' but they didn't have a name for it then."

Pee Wee's countenance, particularly with clarinet in mouth, was a sight to behold. His facial expressions inspired attention. His face was a jazz photographer's dream come true.

He died in February, 1969, just after working with the Tommy Gwaltney group, including me, at Blues Alley in Washington. Pancreatitis, the doctors said.

Charlie Shavers also died shortly after a Blues Alley engagement, as mentioned earlier. As did another great player, trombonist Lou McGarity. Lou suffered a heart attack while appearing at Blues Alley in August, 1971.

Pee Wee Russell was a sweet guy. He never put people down. He always put them up. And make no mistake about it, his fame was well deserved.

Tony Tamburello plays piano beautifully but never worked in bands. Instead, he became a top vocal coach. He was the first coach Tony Bennett had, I believe, and in any event was with Tony as coach and arranger for eighteen years. And Tamburello has written many lyrics that could never be performed. For example:

(Verse) You've been working so long in that factory
      Running that dangerous machine,
      For years and years I have worried,
      Now maybe you know what I mean . . .
(Chorus, to the tune of *Little Girl Blue*)
      Sit there and count your fingers . . .

Tony was also the vocal coach for Bernadine Read, a pretty girl who sang with Fred Waring. When she left Waring to sing in clubs, Tony told her, kiddingly, she couldn't use her real name, she must have a stage name. Tony decided a good name for her would be Bermuda Schwartz.

In the late 1950s, Tamburello wrote an act for her, and Bernadine worked in a number of good rooms including the Blue Angel in New York and the

Ibo Lele Hotel in Port-au-Prince, Haiti. Tony also wrote arrangements for an album she did with a large orchestra conducted by Don Costa. One night she invited pianist Teddy Napoleon and me to hear her new album. It was a good set and included a lovely, slow version of *I Know That You Know*, complete with violins. Teddy couldn't believe it. "That's beautiful," he said, "and to think I used to chase acrobats with that tune!"

Ah yes, Teddy remembered those stage show days, as do I.

When Tony Tamburello was younger, he didn't have enough money to rent a studio for his teaching. He used an old, vanlike paneled truck, with a piano in it, as a studio. He'd tell a piano or vocal student to meet him at two o'clock at Lexington Avenue and 30th Street. The student would take his half-hour or forty-five-minute lesson, and Tony would say, "I've gotta run because I've got another lesson in twenty minutes at 50th Street and Second Avenue." He operated like that all day long.

In the middle 1950s, Tony made *Time* magazine along with a friend of his, the late Tom Murray, an advertising executive. Tony and Tom wrote some tunes with strange lyrics and got some sixty-eight-year-old woman to sing them and record them. The records were terrible and they made a lot of money. One of these songs was *The Sound of Worms*. It began: "There's a new sound underneath the ground, the sound that's made by worms . . ."

Tony is a big man with great talent and a great appetite. One time he got a job at an Italian restaurant in Jersey City playing solo piano for an hour and half on each set. The job paid $85 a week plus dinner every night. When it came time for dinner his first night, Tony says, "Well, I'll have some prosciutto and melon, a plate of rigatoni, three or four sausages on the side, bread, your best Italian salad, and for dessert I'll have spumoni and cookies."

The owner laughed. "For you," he said, "dinner is spaghetti and meatballs."

"But you said dinner and that's the kind of dinner I eat at home," said Tony.

"Well, go home and eat," said the owner, and thus endeth that gig for Tony Tamburello. (This story was told to me by his famous colleague, Tony Bennett.)

Tamburello is known to many as Tony Burello and one time he told me he had a great new tune. "Now hear this," he says, and begins to sing: "Tony Burello you are a swell fellow and I love you. Tony Burello you are a swell fellow and I love you." Now, he says, get the middle part: "Tony Burello you are a swell fellow and I love you." Then he raises his voice and gives the final bars a dramatic reading: "Tony Burello you are a swell fellow and . . . I . . . Love . . . You!"

"Who wrote that," I asked, "your mother?"

"Oh, no," says Tony, "I wrote that one myself."

I worked with Israel Crosby, a great bass player, in Goodman big bands and Goodman sextets during the 1950s.

Israel made his first record when he was only fifteen years old. And quite a debut it was, *Blues of Israel,* with a small group organized by John Hammond and led by Gene Krupa. He was forty-three when he died of a blood clot on his heart in August, 1962. He was working with pianist George Shearing at the time and had taken a two-week leave of absence from the Shearing group to have his blinding headaches and blurred vision checked out in a VA hospital in his hometown, Chicago. After his death, Shearing had it right when he said, "He played bass parts that were so beautiful. You could never write bass parts as good. He was one of the most inspiring musicians I ever worked with."

Israel Crosby was also quite a character. I roomed with him once and I know.

On a flight with the Goodman band one night, he was in a window seat next to trombonist Jack Rains. He suddenly said to Jack, "Hey man, those people down there look like tiny little ants!" Jack replied, "Hey, man, they *are* ants. We haven't taken off yet!"

Another time we had a flight to Pittsburgh and had chartered a bus to pick us up at the airport and take us to Harrisburg, about 100 miles away. We couldn't get a flight directly to Harrisburg. Israel had consumed more than his share of beers and was well juiced, so after the plane landed we woke him up and managed to get him and his bass on the bus. I was sitting next to him and the bus was going about 90 miles an hour on the Pennsylvania Turnpike. After about fifteen minutes he stirred and said, "Hey, man, this is the longest goddamn runway I've ever been on in my life!"

And one morning in Chicago, when the Goodman band had to catch an airplane, everyone was on the bus ready to take off for the airport when road manager Bill Kratt said he couldn't find Israel. It was 9 A.M. and he wasn't in his room. Suddenly, someone noticed Israel leaning out of a window on the fourth or fifth floor, and Kratt yelled, "What are you doing? Come on down." He looked at us and said, "How brown now cow?" Don't ask me why, but that's all he said. He closed the window and joined us in five minutes. He apparently had been taking a shower when Kratt called his room.

You never knew what the delightfully different Israel Crosby might say. But you could always be certain about his bass playing. It was always excellent.

Nick Travis was a marvelous first trumpet player who worked with many name bands including Woody Herman, Ray McKinley, Benny Goodman, Tommy Dorsey, and Sauter-Finegan before going on NBC staff. He was only thirty-nine when he died in 1964.

While we were working with Benny at the Waldorf, he told me that he had saved money for nearly a year to buy the best color TV available. But he had it only one week. Seems his sister came over to see the set and brought her son, about seven years old. Nick turned on Hopalong Cassidy for the kid and went into the dining room to eat. On the TV, someone was saying, "I think we've got Hoppy back in the cave and he doesn't have a gun." Suddenly, the kid yells, "Here's my gun, Hoppy," and throws a toy pistol into the TV tube and the whole thing exploded. Nick's nephew was okay but there was no more picture tube.

Lee Castaldo, who became Lee Castle, was a fine trumpet player who gained fame working with big bands during the late 1930s and early 1940s. Many years later, Lee led "The Tommy Dorsey Orchestra" and "The Jimmy Dorsey Orchestra" (sounds anachronistic, doesn't it?). When I worked with Lee, he was always complaining about his chops. We were with a band at the Paramount Theater in New York and one day he heard that I was going to a nearby music store. "If you're going to Manny's," he said, "pick me up a box of fifty lips."

Lee is one of the few musicians I know who seemed to be able to get along just fine with Tommy Dorsey. That wasn't easy. Ask any former Dorsey sideman. A typical Dorsey bandstand activity was standing in front of his band, facing his players, with fists clenched, yelling through gritted teeth, "RELAX, RELAX, RELAX!"

Lee worked with many prominent bands including Artie Shaw, Benny Goodman, Red Norvo, Glenn Miller, Jack Teagarden, Will Bradley, and Joe Venuti. And like anyone who has worked with Venuti, he tells some fascinating Venuti stories.

Venuti was the great violinist who was swinging his tail off in the 1920s long before swing became a household word. And until his death in 1978,

My First L-5 Gibson.
I was seventeen years
old and playing in an
orchestra at Flushing
High School, Long
Island, New York, when
this was taken in 1936.

Will Bradley. Nice guy
and superior trombonist
who did not tolerate
sloppy playing in his
band. (Institute of Jazz
Studies.)

Beside the band bus. *Standing, from left:* Steve Lipkins, Alec Fila, me, Lee Castaldo, Mahlon Clark, Jim Emert, Will Bradley, Terry Allen, and, I think, Al Klink. *Front:* Art Mendelsohn, Ray McKinley, Doc Goldberg, Bobby Holt, Peanuts Hucko. And that's band manager Doc Richardson hanging out the bus window. (Courtesy of Will Bradley.)

Backstage somewhere in 1941. Bradley band members. *Standing, from left:* Mahlon Clark, Will Bradley, Steve Lipkins, Art Rollini (with sax), Terry Allen. *Seated:* Felix Giobbe, Lee Castaldo, Ralph Muzzillo, Jim Emert (face hidden), Les Robinson, Pete Mondello, Bill Corti, me, Billy Maxted. (Courtesy of Will Bradley.)

Dancing at the Astor. Lynn Gardner sings with the Bradley band at the Hotel Astor in New York, 1941. *From left:* trumpets: Ralph Muzzillo, Steve Lipkins, Lee Castaldo (who became Lee Castle); trombones: Bill Corti, Jim Emert; saxophones: John Hayes, Art Rollini, Les Robinson, Mahlon Clark, Pete Mondello (behind Gardner); rhythm: drummer Ray McKinley, me, bassist Felix Giobbe, pianist Billy Maxted; singer Terry Allen is seated to my left. (Courtesy of Will Bradley.)

Freddie Slack. A close friend and fascinating character who said and did the damnedest things. Who else but Freddie would have a pet lion? Despite his faults, I loved the guy. (Frank Driggs Collection.)

A New Bradley Band. By late 1941, after Freddie Slack and Ray McKinley left to start their own bands, Will Bradley had a new band. I remained, as did singers Terry Allen and Lynn Gardner (seated, front left). Shelly Manne, eighteen, replaced McKinley, and others in the rhythm section were pianist Billy Maxted and bassist Marty Brown. *From left:* saxophones: Ray Schultz, Phil Gomez, Ray Beller, Sal Augusta, Bob Wertz; trombones: Irv Dinkin, Leonard Ray, and Bradley in front; trumpets: Max Greer, Tony Faso, and Shorty Rogers, who like Manne became famous later. That's road manager Frank Harper in the wings, top right. (Frank Driggs Collection.)

My Super 400. Doc Goldberg is the bass player. This must have been a rehearsal because we are in different suits. This guitar is a Gibson Super 400. The photo is dated 1941. Doc later worked with Glenn Miller. (Frank Driggs Collection.)

Bob Chester. One of the unsung heroes of the big band days. When I was with him, his band could certainly swing, but we kept losing key musicians because of all the one-nighters. (Frank Driggs Collection.)

Lynn Gardner. When I was twenty-one and with the Bradley band, my one and only girl was Lynn, the band's nineteen-year-old singer. (Frank Driggs Collection.)

Artie Shaw. An exceptional clarinet player with an exceptional ear. He once stopped a band rehearsal because he said my G string (the weakest string on the guitar) was a little flat. And he was right. (Institute of Jazz Studies.)

Teddy Powell. A big-hearted guy and some of his players took advantage of this fact. He had an excellent band in 1942, but the recording ban kept it from getting the national attention it deserved. (Institute of Jazz Studies.)

Stan Kenton. I will always cherish my time with Kenton's band. Anyone who puts Stan or his music down gets an argument from me. (Courtesy of Mae Scanlan.)

Boyd Raeburn. Too bad his band, a great one in many ways, never made it. It should have. (Institute of Jazz Studies.)

Shelly Manne. A good friend and a marvelous drummer.

Coleman Hawkins and Charlie Shavers. The granddaddy of tenor sax playing with one of the greatest of all trumpet players. (Institute of Jazz Studies.)

Long lines for Benny. When the Goodman Sextet played New York's Basin Street Club in 1954, the lines waiting to get in were always long. Working with Benny, you became accustomed to standing-room-only crowds. (Frank Driggs Collection.)

Will Bradley's Band. In front of the Steel Pier in Atlantic City, 1939 or 1940. Poster in the center bills Bradley as "The Boy with the Horn" and Ray McKinley as "The Kid with the Drums." *From left:* Sam Sachelle, tenor sax; Bill Corti, trombone; Art Mendelsohn, alto sax; Freddie Slack, piano; Doc Goldberg, bass; Joe Wiedman, trumpet; Louise Tobin, singer; Will Bradley; Ray McKinley, drums; me; Steve Lipkins, trumpet; Jimmy Valentine, singer; Al Mitchell, trumpet; Nick Ciazza, tenor sax; Jim Emert, trombone; Jo Jo Huffman, alto sax and clarinet. (Frank Driggs Collection.)

Boyd Raeburn's *big* big band.
Here's the Raeburn band at VPI
in Blacksburg, Virginia, in 1947,
I think. *From left:* singers Jay
Johnson and Ginny Powell; Ray
Rossi, piano; Joe Burreice, bass;
Lloyd Otto, French horn; Vince
De Mino, French horn; Irv Kluger,
drums; Sam Spumberg, baritone
sax, clarinet; me (behind the
mike); Shirley Thompson, tenor
sax, bassoon, bass clarinet; Boyd
Raeburn, with bass sax; Buddy
DeFranco, clarinet; Wes Hensel,
trumpet; Leon Cox, trombone; Pete
Candoli, trumpet; Jerry Sanfino,
alto sax; Dick Noel, trombone;
Bernie Glow, trumpet; Frankie
Socolow, tenor sax; Gordon
Boswell, trumpet; Hal Smith,
trombone; Hy Mandel, baritone
sax. (Frank Driggs Collection.)

Buck Clayton. I loved Buck Clayton, a great musician and delightful guy. (Frank Driggs Collection.)

Gene Krupa. An ardently religious man, well liked by everyone who knew him. There'll never be another Gene Krupa.

Vic Dickenson. He talked, on the trombone, with great power and wit, and the accent was his own. (Institute of Jazz Studies.)

The Benny Goodman Sextet in 1954. The best small group I ever worked with, at Basin Street, New York City: pianist Mel Powell, Benny, me, trumpeter Charlie Shavers, bassist Israel Crosby, and drummer Morey Feld. (Frank Driggs Collection.)

With Benny Goodman at the Waldorf. This is March, 1957, at the Waldorf-Astoria in New York. *From left:* Mel Powell, piano; Irv Manning, bass; Mousey Alexander, drums; me; Buck Clayton, Jimmy Maxwell, Nick Travis, trumpets; Rex Peer, Eddie Bert, trombones; Budd Johnson, Red Press, Al Block, saxes (the other saxophonist, Sol Schilinger, not shown, is behind Benny). (Courtesy of Warren Hicks and Frank Driggs.)

Budd Johnson (with Benny Goodman). At a Singapore bar, he was acceptable, I was not. "How do you like it?" Budd asked me. (Frank Driggs Collection.)

With Ruby Braff, 1954. This was taken in August, 1954, at the Village Vanguard in New York. Braff's swinging group included clarinetist Pee Wee Russell, bassist Walter Page, and pianist Nat Pierce. (Photo by Popsie Randolph, Frank Driggs Collection.)

Me and Pee Wee. Clarinetist Pee Wee Russell was a sweet guy who never put people down, and who played music with conviction and heart. (Photo by Popsie Randolph, Frank Driggs Collection.)

Billy Butterfield. He had a fat tone, great range, and he wailed loud and clear. (Institute of Jazz Studies.)

Pat Kidney Jordan. Patty was twenty-seven when this was taken, before we met. If this were a color picture, you'd see she's a redhead.

A gift from Julie. This was Christmas Eve, 1964, and as I arrived home at 2 A.M. from a gig, Julie's flash bulb caught me by surprise. She had stayed up late to present her Christmas card and gift to me.

With Jimmy Rushing. Count Basie's great singer, the original "Mr. Five by Five," holds the mike for a guitar solo at Blues Alley in Washington, 1968.

With "Hot Jazz." Part of Brooks Tegler's swinging group at the 219 Club in Alexandria, Virginia, 1988. *From left:* John Cocuzzi on vibes, me, Brooks, and trumpet player Clyde Hunt. (Photo by Mae Scanlan.)

Off to the islands. Boarding the *Caribe* with Patty for a ten-day cruise to Haiti, Puerto Rico, Caneel Bay, St. Thomas, and the Bahamas in 1978. This was the only cruise ship ever to sail from Alexandria, Virginia.

Patty and me, 1988. This was taken shortly after we celebrated our twenty-fifth wedding anniversary. (Photo by Mae Scanlan.)

he swung more than any other fiddler in the world. Venuti is also the central character in many famous jazz tales, and Lord only knows how many of them are true. I once asked Joe if all those wild stories about him were true, and he said some were and some were not, and he added this: "I'll tell you one thing, Steve, true or not, don't ever tell a story if it isn't funny."

So maybe Venuti did or did not smash a violin over the head of a clubowner who was bugging him. And who knows if he really chopped up some small trees and brought them into a ballroom to build a fire because it was too cold in there? And did he really give Wingy Manone one cufflink for Christmas? But Lee Castaldo swore the following story *is* true.

It involves a college prom somewhere in Texas in the 1930s. The Venuti band was booked to play as the relief band to Paul Whiteman's fancy orchestra. The prom was in the college gym with a bandstand at each end. Whiteman had a three-foot-long baton with batteries in the handle and a small light bulb at the pointer end. After the first set ended, Whiteman pulled out a six gun, fired a shot in the air Texas-style, then yelled, "Take it away, Joe!"

As Whiteman's orchestra, in white tie yet, moved off and Venuti's smaller, somewhat ragged looking group began to play, Joe left the stand. When he got back he held a fifteen-foot clothesline stick with a sixty-watt bulb tied at the end, corded and plugged into a socket on stage. He led his band with that contraption, and when the set ended he picked up a shotgun, fired two blasts toward the ceiling, and yelled, "Take it away, Paul!"

With that same band, Lee said that one time on a tour of one-nighters they pulled the bus up to a hotel in Providence, Rhode Island, about 3 A.M. Everyone was dead tired but there was to be no rest for the Venuti band in that hotel that night. Venuti had gone to the desk and discovered the price of rooms was out of sight for his struggling group of swingers. "How about a special rate?" he asked the clerk. "There are sixteen of us." But there was no special rate. Joe was furious. As he left, he gave the clerk one of his famous raspberries—Venuti was the undisputed raspberry-giving champ—and screamed: "For thirty bucks a night you could at least wear a clean shirt!"

One October day in 1938 I was on Long Island Sound in a twenty-eight-foot sailboat with a friend of mine, now Admiral Dugald Neill, when the famous New England hurricane of '38 struck. We had just a five-horsepower outboard auxiliary motor we always brought along to be used in case the wind died down. Die down it didn't! We were in the middle of the sound until 10:30 at night, with the mainsail ripped, no sea anchor, and the boat swamped. I thought we'd never get back.

Years later, I was talking about this experience with Georgie Auld, who also remembered that 1938 hurricane well. Auld, one of the best tenor saxophone players, was with Bunny Berigan's band then, working a job on the roof garden of the Brunswick Hotel in Boston. He said that the band was swinging, and there were many dancing when this hurricane ripped the roof off the whole hotel. The rain poured in, huge pieces of debris fell all over the dance floor and the bandstand, people were screaming high notes that even Berigan's trumpet couldn't reach, and the Berigan band's engagement at the Brunswick ended in seconds flat.

In the early 1950s, I worked in television production at NBC in New York for about seven months while I gigged at night. I thought TV production was something I could learn and fall back on if the music business got too impossible. I left when they cut out the deadwood, because I was part of the deadwood. My TV production "career" didn't last long because live shows were being replaced by filmed shows, and outside decorators and designers were hired instead of NBC staff. They were cheaper.

One day while chatting with Bob Gable, whom I worked with at NBC, I mentioned Mel Tormé. Bob immediately said he didn't like him, that he was a little wise guy. I said, "Well, I don't know him but I do know he's a great singer, writes wonderful tunes, and plays piano, too." Then Gable told me his experience with Tormé.

NBC has sent Bob to Los Angeles to arrange a television setting and he was having dinner with one of the NBC people in what Gable described as "a nice little joint, nothing fancy" and Mel Tormé was the featured attraction. The guy with Bob knew Tormé and the singer joined them between sets. Bob said that Tormé talked endlessly about when he did this, when he did that, when he wrote this song and that song, how he improved Judy Garland's singing, and on and on. Finally, annoyed by all this, Bob said, with gritted teeth, "Yeah, but what are you doing *now*?"

Mel cut him down quickly. "Oh," he said, "I'm over at Warner Brothers making *Good News*. I just do this on weekends for fun because a friend of mine owns this place."

To my mind, Tormé is the best. I think his singing is marvelous. I've thought so since I heard his Mel-Tones group in the 1940s. Remember when they called him "The Velvet Fog?" He sings the way a fine musician plays. He can even wail with Ella.

Irv Greenberg, a big, fat, jolly guy who sold Ford automobiles in Norfolk, Virginia, was a great jazz enthusiast. A year or so before he died of a heart attack he came to the Manassas Jazz Festival. It was his first visit to Manassas and he had arrived the night before. As we were having a drink in the hospitality suite of the hotel a few hours before the concert was to begin, Irv told me his impressions of Manassas: "It's a nice, quiet, little town. I like the way it's laid out. But last night I heard some funny noises and got scared. I tried to call the police but found out they had an unlisted number. Then this morning I knew they had a police department because I saw a squad car across the street and it said Manassas No. 1."

Clarinetist Tommy Gwaltney told me that in the early 1950s in Norfolk there was a place where sessions were held regularly. All jazz musicians were invited to drop by and sit in. With a horn, you went in the back way and didn't have to pay admission and you could also drink all the beer or Coke you wanted. One night Tommy brought Irv Greenberg in with him, but since Irv was not carrying a horn, a big black guy challenged him, "What do you play, man?"

Thinking quickly, Irv replied, "Oh, I play vibes, man, and you can't carry vibes."

Almost immediately a little black guy went somewhere and was soon rolling out an old set of vibes. "Here, man," he said, "here's a nice set of vibes." Irv froze, but again thought quickly. Irv knew that on vibes the notes are laid out loosely with a string holding them on each end. Irv went plink plink on the vibes and said: "Man, these vibes are loose! Man, I can't play loose vibes!" And the big black guy said to the little black guy, "Yeah, man, get them out of here. You know the man can't play loose vibes!"

After one of the Manassas Jazz Festivals, one Sunday morning a group of musicians and some wives had brunch at festival producer Johnson (Fat Cat) McRee's home. Margie Singleton, wife of the late Zutty Singleton, the famous drummer from New Orleans who worked with Louis Armstrong, Sidney Bechet, Fats Waller, Roy Eldridge and you name them, was telling my wife Patty about "the old days."

She said at one time she and Zutty had an apartment in a converted house run by a Puerto Rican lady and she was a tough landlady. One day she told them, "If you don't pay your rent by Sunday your stuff is out on the street Monday morning!"

Zutty had a gig that Saturday night and with that gig and with what they had saved they would be able to pay the rent on Sunday with some left over. But what could have been left over wasn't. A few days later, after a few drinks, Zutty passed a pet shop and saw a very expensive dog that he was certain Margie would love.

When he arrived home with his beautiful present and explained that he had spent all his money, Margie said, "That's a bringdown."

Bringdown became the dog's name. And because she didn't want an expensive dog to catch cold, Margie made a sweater for the dog by cutting off an arm of a coat sweater she had.

The Singletons took Bringdown on the road for many years, and he was well known to all musicians who worked with Zutty. When Bringdown was too old to travel, the only people he would stay with were the Basies. Count Basie and his wife were very fond of Bringdown and when he died and was buried in a New York dog cemetery, he became, no doubt, the only dog in history that had the Count Basie band play at his funeral!

Fat Cat McRee, an accountant by profession and a jazz nut by avocation, produced his last Manassas Jazz Festival in December, 1989. Years before he had lost a great deal of weight and joked that he ought to be called Skinny Cat, not Fat Cat. In late January, 1990, he went to sleep one night and never woke up. He was sixty-seven. At his funeral in Manassas, some musicians brought their horns (I was talked into bringing my guitar) but church people said playing jazz at a funeral wouldn't be dignified, or something. Well, I know if it had been up to Fat Cat, he would have had a Dixieland band roaring at the funeral. And, if it could have been possible, he would have joined in. On kazoo.

One bandleader I certainly enjoyed working for was Richard Maltby. I worked for him on a number of occasions during the 1950s and he was unquestionably one of the kindest people in the music business or any other business. Quite an arranger, too. For example, he did *Six Flats Unfurnished* for Benny Goodman's band in 1942. Musicians have many stories about Maltby to prove what a great guy he was, and here's one of mine.

"Chasie"—I forgot his full name—played tenor saxophone well and got a good salary in Maltby's band, but he had to support an ailing mother in Brooklyn and a young sister in school who was twelve or thirteen. He sent nearly his whole salary home every week. He could pay his hotel bill and buy food and that was about all. One night Maltby told me he noticed that Chasie never went out drinking with the guys, never even had a beer or two. I told Maltby that was because he didn't have any money and he was proud. Maltby said, "Well, he needs more money then." So Maltby got on the phone and talked to his New York accounting office about raising Chasie's salary. He was told it couldn't be done. Maltby replied, "Okay, give him a $25 a week raise and take it out of my check." I was the only member of the band who knew Maltby had done that. He said he never told anybody else about it and didn't want anyone to know. I never heard of any other bandleader doing such a thing. Usually, if a musician can't make it financially, he quits when he can't get a raise and another player is easily found. But Maltby was different. And rare.

When I was working with Maltby's eighteen-piece orchestra in the Cafe Rouge at the Statler Hotel in New York, I often had dinner with Kenny Arzburger, who played baritone sax and bass clarinet with Maltby. At the Statler, Kenny usually ordered spaghetti with marijuana sauce. And the waitress never batted an eye.

Another memory from my days with Maltby. At ten o'clock one morning I was having breakfast and waiting for some other members of the band to arrive at Charlie's Tavern, where the Maltby bus was to pick us up for a tour. A young kid, with visible shakes, came in and someone said he was with Woody Herman's band. "Gimme a shot of bourbon, gimme a shot of bourbon," he told the bartender who was polishing glasses and was just about to open the bar. "Just a second, don't be nervous," said the bartender. "Don't be nervous?" said the kid, "You might as well tell me don't be Jewish! Gimme a shot!"

He had one or two shots and stopped shaking. He didn't look or seem like a drunk. He'd probably been to a party the night before and had more than was his custom.

But too much drinking is a problem for many musicians. I've seen it ruin more than one career. But sometimes a man can cut down on the juice and straighten himself out. A fine alto saxophone player from Boston—who shall be nameless here—is a case in point.

One night in 1958 in Junior's Bar, when he was about twenty-four years old, he stumbled over to my table, drunk. "Hey, Steve," he mumbled, "you're just in time to buy me a drink. I had a hazelnut and a grape today. I'm glad I've eaten."

I was having a special plate of roast beef, French fried potatoes, peas and carrots. The price was only about $1.50. "Hey," he said, "can I have one of those French fries?"

"Have a plate of the same thing," I said, and insisted.

He ate, had another drink, and said, sadly, "You know, you can always ask somebody to buy you a drink but you can't ask anybody to buy you some food 'cause then you know you've hit bottom."

"Well, I don't feel that way about you," I told him. "I can give you five dollars. Why don't you go home (he lived on Tenth Avenue over a grocery store that didn't close until 4 A.M.) and go to that store below and buy some cornflakes and sugar and milk and orange juice and have breakfast in the morning." He thought it was a great idea and resolved to try to get normal.

A few days later at Nola studios I was filling in for one rehearsal with a new band Frankie Carle was organizing for the road when Carle asked me if I knew anyone who could play lead alto or third alto. I said, sure, thinking of my friend from Boston. "He's a helluva player," I told Carle. "Fine," said Carle, "tell him there's a rehearsal tomorrow at three o'clock."

That evening I found him in Junior's. He looked okay and told me he had straightened up. But he never showed up for the rehearsal. He told me later that he didn't wake up until four o'clock.

A few weeks later I was having dinner with Bobby Gefaell and Hal McIntyre, the bandleader, and discovered that McIntyre was looking for some guys for the road. I told Hal all about my alto saxophone friend, and Hal said he'd give him a chance.

The chance paid off. The saxophonist cut out the booze, got the job, and was with McIntyre for more than three months on the road.

Ironically, it was my friend's first good chance in several years and it ended, well, tragically. The leader died. McIntyre, standout lead alto player for Glenn Miller and a gentleman well liked by his players, died in 1959 of smoke inhalation from a fire in his Los Angeles apartment caused by a cigarette.

Last I heard of the alto player from Boston he was living in a hotel off Broadway, working full time, and was still off the sauce. And I wonder if he's still nuts about baseball. When I knew him he was always talking about Ted Williams and he played on the Charlie's Tavern softball team. Softball teams representing different taverns and several bands played in Central Park in those days. Earl Swope, who played trombone with Boyd Raeburn, Buddy Rich, Woody Herman, and Jimmy Dorsey, was one of the star players, which was understandable since he once played for a Washington Senators farm club. Earl died in 1968 at the age of forty-five. His younger brother Rob, who also played trombone with top bands—he replaced Earl in Buddy Rich's 1947 band and went on to work with Gene Krupa and Elliot Lawrence and Jimmy Dorsey—died the year before, 1967, at forty. The Swope brothers were from Washington, D.C.

Like many others, I enjoy singing the lyrics of Johnny Mercer. His words are singable and they make sense. He was one of the two or three best lyric writers ever. Maybe *the* best. He wrote the words to so many standards most anyone who cares about American popular music knows. *That Old Black Magic, Fools Rush In, Jeepers Creepers* (inspired, Mercer said, by the large eyes of Helen Ward, "peepers" that "hypnotize," as his words contend), *Laura, Goody Goody, Come Rain or Come Shine, I Thought About You, Blues in the Night, I Wanna Be Around, You Must Have Been a Beautiful Baby, Dream, Too Marvelous for Words, Skylark, Days of Wine and Roses,* and what seems like a zillion others.

I think Alec Wilder had it right in his fine 1972 book with James T. Maher, *American Popular Song,* when he said this: "There is a great difference between the quality of a song written by a performer and one written by a nonperformer. I believe that one of the reasons John Mercer's lyrics have an added zest, a crackle and a shine to them, is that he probably sings them as he writes them."

And Johnny Mercer could certainly sing! As Ray McKinley said to me about Mercer years ago: "Yeah, he's got a voice like a gila monster from the Stone Age and he's the best singer in the world."

Mercer was from Savannah, Georgia, and the grandson of a Confederate colonel. In the 1987 book *Singers & the Song,* Gene Lees writes, "Of all the awards [Mercer] got in his life, he was proudest of one he received in 1944: a black boys club in Chicago voted him the outstanding young Negro singer of the year."

Mercer had countless friends in the world of music. And some of his delightful verse was seen only by those friends who received lengthy light verse, seventy lines or more, from Mercer at Christmas time instead of the usual card. Having seen the poems sent to Helen Ward, described by writer James T. Maher as "the quintessential big band singer," and her husband, Bill Savory, I can assure the reader that these unpublished gems rank right up there with Johnny's great song lyrics.

Bill is probably best known to jazz fans as the radio and Columbia Records engineer who recorded and edited Benny Goodman's 1937–38 broadcast recordings. As assistant chief of research and development at Columbia, he was also involved in the development of the LP (long-playing) record.

Gene Krupa was a Catholic. Indeed, as a young man, he had wanted to study for the priesthood. In 1953, after the Goodman band arrived in Washington by plane early in the morning for a concert that night, we were in a bus going from the airport to the Sheraton-Park Hotel shortly before 6 A.M. when Krupa asked to driver to stop the bus a block or so from the hotel. He had noticed the St. Thomas Catholic Church. "Let me off," he said, "I'll go to six o'clock mass, and then I won't have to get up again this morning."

It must be said, too, that Gene Krupa was no "dope fiend" as too many unknowing people seemed to think because of his jail sentence in 1943. He may have used a little marijuana on occasion, but he was jailed on a bum rap, "contributing to the delinquency of a minor."

The bandboy involved was under eighteen and happened to be in Krupa's hotel room discussing something or other when the phone rang. The kid took the call and told Krupa it was one of the musicians who was in the lobby, saying that a couple of cops had asked for Gene's room number and were on their way up. Krupa immediately gave the kid a small package of marijuana and told him to throw it out on the parking lot.

As the cops got off the elevator, the kid was running down the hall toward a window overlooking the parking lot. They grabbed the package from the kid, saw what it was, and asked him where he got it. He told them that Gene Krupa had given it to him.

Gene told the cops the kid wouldn't use it, he was only going to throw it out. "How do you know?" one of the cops said to Gene.

Gene should have thrown it down the toilet. Maybe he figured if it was tossed on the parking lot he could go down and get it later, I don't know. In any event, Gene Krupa was never a junkie, never involved with hard drugs, and wasn't making a delinquent out of his bandboy. He was a God-fearing, ardently religious man and well liked by everyone who knew him.

I played with a big pickup band one night in Connecticut in 1972, a band composed mainly of swing era veterans. It was a kind of nostalgia night, bringing back the sounds of swing one more time. Helen Ward was there, and so were Ray McKinley and Gene Krupa.

At dinner between shows, Gene told Ray and me, very confidentially, that he was almost dead. He had leukemia. He couldn't drink, couldn't smoke, and had to follow a certain diet. But he looked good and played well, whipping through *Wire Brush Stomp* as he had more than thirty years before. Gene died the following year.

Helen said to me that night, "There'll never be another Gene Krupa." And she's right. So, Buddy Rich was faster. But as Rich said, "No one ever got a sound from a snare drum like Gene."

8

"I'm Dig," Said Zoot

Beale Riddle, a jazz enthusiast and record collector who died in 1984, believed that jazz musicians have a quicker wit than is to be found in most trades and professions. He suggested that this may be due to the fact that jazz musicians are involved with improvisation all the time in their work, thus the one-liner is a natural instinct. Maybe he was right. In any event, a few examples of jazz musician wit to support his theory.

Clarinetist Hank D'Amico and guitarist Carl Kress, two superior musicians no longer with us, had an hour to wait for their train one day at the Long Island railroad station in New York City. So naturally they headed for the Savarin bar in the station. Naturally because—as anyone who knew these two gentlemen can tell you—they liked a taste. And next to Carl at the bar that day was a guy weaving from side to side, leaning on the bar with his hands. His eyes were almost completely closed. Carl turned to him and asked: "Is this your first crossing?"

At the bar in a jazz club, a young jazz enthusiast, snapping his fingers to the music on the juke box, and in general trying to be the hippest, was standing beside tenor saxophonist Zoot Sims. As an attractive girl passed by, he said to Zoot: "Hey, man, hip that groovy chick."
And Zoot replied: "I'm dig!"

In the summer of 1951, or maybe it was the summer of 1952, I signed a contract to play on singer James Melton's television show. The conductor was the late David Broekman, an excellent musician, legitimate that is. There were about thirty-five men in the orchestra. Bunny Shawker was the drummer. I always liked Bunny. He loved baseball almost as much as he loved the drums, and he was not without wit. During a rehearsal one day, we were playing an up-tempo piece for a tap dancer. Brokeman stopped us all at one point and said to Shawker: "Drummer, look at me, watch the baton!" Bunny said: "Oh, I'm sorry, I thought you wanted this the same tempo all the way through!"

Gene McCoy, a Washington, D.C., businessman who loves jazz, was in Jimmy Ryan's in New York listening to trumpet player Max Kaminsky play some of his honest, no-nonsense kind of music. As Kaminsky left the bandstand and passed McCoy's table, Gene said, "Hey, Max, how long have you been playing jazz? Just curious."

Little Max said, "Just a moment," hustled back to the bandstand, opened the piano bench and was soon back with his autobiography, *My Life in Jazz.* "What's your name?" he asked McCoy. McCoy told him, and Max took out a pen and wrote in the book: "To Gene McCoy, one of my favorite fans, Max Kaminsky." He handed the book to Gene and said, "That'll be five dollars." So Gene paid him the five dollars and took the book.

Eddie Condon was a deservedly famous character and master of the quick quip. You may remember that it was Eddie who said of French jazz critics: "How can they tell us about jazz? Do we tell them how to stomp on a grape?" But, as is well known, Eddie drank too much. I saw him one afternoon at a Manassas Jazz Festival about two years before he died. He was impeccably dressed in a Brooks Brothers suit, but he was drunk. He came up to me and said, "Hey, how you doin', still blowing that hot horn?"

I said, "No, Eddie, I play guitar, you know that."

"Hey, I think I do know that," he mumbled.

"Yes, Eddie," I said, "I think you do, too, and it's nice seeing you again."

It was sad. I wondered how this master of the four-string tenor guitar could perform on stage that day. (Eddie was a fine banjo player, and when guitar replaced the banjo in jazz bands in the early 1930s he found it easier to switch to the tenor guitar than to learn the six-string guitar.) Condon was a delightful, witty guy, quick to help his fellow man and fight the good fight, a musician who did a great deal to get jazz serious attention and proper recognition. He knew me but thought I was a trumpet player. When he went on stage with his group that day, he sat down, kicked off the tempo, the band started to play, and he promptly leaned over his guitar and fell asleep.

Marshall Brown, the late valve trombonist, told me the following story about Eddie Condon.

About twenty years ago, Condon was in the hospital for reasons deeply involved with alcohol. His wife, Phyllis, and a friend of Eddie's had prepared a list of about twenty-five musicians Condon knew or knew about who had died strictly from drinking too much alcohol. Phyllis went to the hospital and said, "Eddie, please, look at this list."

Eddie looked at the list of jazz all-stars and handed it back to Phyllis. "No drummer," he said.

Another Marshall Brown story about Eddie follows.

When Eddie was in the hospital at death's edge, there was a benefit concert for him at Carnegie Hall. It picked up about $12,000 for his wife. Some wondered about the concert because the Condons certainly didn't seem in need, and when Eddie recovered he found that some people wouldn't even talk to him because of that benefit concert.

Eddie asked Brown: "Do they want me to give the money back just because I didn't die on schedule?"

You can believe it or not, but once upon a time a couple of wits started the No Hope Music Publishing Company of New Hope, Pennsylvania. They published a song entitled *When You're in Love, Everybody's Jewish.* I remember only the last line: "The whole world's Jewish when you're in love!"

Helen Ward, the singer with Benny Goodman's first band, told me that when Vido Musso first joined the Goodman band in 1936 he couldn't read music very well. But when he played his first chorus with the band it was so good that Benny said "play another" and then "play another" again. And on the next tune, Benny jumped off the bandstand in the ballroom and just stood there listening to Vido solo.

When young Vido, an immigrant from Sicily who spoke broken English, explained his reading problems to Benny, he said it wasn't the notes that troubled him it was "the res-tez." Benny had his excellent lead alto player Hymie Schertzer give Vido private reading lessons.

In the first Goodman band Vido got away with not reading well because his ear was so quick. At a rehearsal when new arrangements would be brought in, Benny might say something like "at letter H change the B-flat to a G," but Vido didn't bother. So when he left the band there were many arrangements in his book with the wrong notes. He also hadn't bothered to mark the softer and louder dynamics anywhere. I'm told that when Babe

Russin came in to replace Vido, he played the wrong notes on every tune. Benny asked, "What's the matter? Can't you read anymore?" Russin was a fine reader. "I'm playing what's here," Babe explained, and they had to go through every chart in the book and make the proper changes, the ones Vido Musso had never bothered to make.

One night Gerry Mulligan eyed a beautiful girl in Charlie's Tavern. He asked some of the guys who she was, and somebody told him not to bother, that he would have no chance because she only liked Italians. Mulligan, a freckle-faced, redheaded Irishman, said that's okay because I'll tell her I'm Italian. He seemed to be making out fine with the object of his affection until she told him "I don't think you're Italian at all. Say something Italian."

Gerry said: "Vido Musso."

(I'm sure Gerry knows much more Italian now. He's married to Italian writer-photographer Franca Rota, whom he met in Milan.)

At a party one night in Washington, I was playing a tune on guitar and said to myself, wait a minute, that's the wrong chord. I tried other chords, again and again, and none sounded right. Guitarist Charlie Byrd was observing. "Keep looking, Steve," he said, "it's on there!"

Saul Glenby, an amateur guitar player who inherited the Venida hairnet business, used to sit on Ocean Beach, Fire Island, strumming a uke, making up new lyrics to old tunes. He had an automobile rear view mirror screwed to the arm of his beachchair so he wouldn't miss any of the chicks strolling by behind him. One lyric he and Bill Arnold created was to the tune of *The Last Time I Saw Paris*. It began: "The last time I saw Morris, he called himself Maurice. He used to hev a tailor shop, now he's ah French modiste . . ."

Ernie Wilkins wrote great arrangements for Tommy Dorsey, Count Basie, Harry James, and many other bands. In the late 1950s, Nat Pierce had a rehearsal band that got together every Wednesday in the Nola studios on Broadway. It was a terrific band composed mainly of CBS and NBC studio musicians who seldom had the chance to play the kind of music this rehearsal band played, including some wild-ass arrangements by Nat, Ernie, and Bill Potts, who were then all writing for Basie. One day when I was there to listen, Ernie submitted a new arrangement. "Okay, all the hot players please assemble and try this," said Nat. The brass players started to run down their parts, and, as the trumpets got higher and higher and began to screech and scream, I said to Nat, "What the hell is that?" He laughed and held up the piano chart so I could see the title. The title was *Goodbye, Mr. Chops.* (The guys played it well but I had the feeling Ernie was thinking of Cat Anderson and Maynard Ferguson when he wrote it.)

"Can you read?" I'm told someone asked the great Louis Armstrong. "Sure," said Louis, "just good enough so it doesn't hurt my playing."

When Count Basie was about to work the Waldorf-Astoria's Starlight Roof twenty-five years ago, someone said they were going to change the name of the hotel to the Waildorf Hotel. I liked that line and a few nights later I was in Jimmy Ryan's on 52nd Street, sitting right next to the bandstand listening to the Sidney and Wilbur DeParis band. Between sets, the piano player, an old veteran, sat next to us and I said to him, "Did you know that Count Basie is scheduled to go into the Waldorf in a week or so?" He said, "You kiddin'," I said, "Yeah, and they're going to change the name of the hotel." I was about to lay that Waildorf line on him when he said, "They going to call it the Woodside?" He beat me to the punch and cut me down!

   (The Woodside was a Harlem hotel where Basie band members lived, and rehearsed, in the basement, when the band first came to New York. Thus the early Basie swinger *Jumpin' at the Woodside.*)

I worked with trumpet player Ernie Figueroa in Freddie Slack's band. Ernie combed his hair straight back and used lots of greasy kid stuff. "I love this goo," he said to me one time. "The other day a fly landed on my hair and slipped to suicide."

About fifteen years ago I thought clarinetist Tommy Gwaltney and I would have a group working at a restaurant called The Whale and Bull. But the job didn't materialize. One night my wife was telling drummer Eddie Phyfe about it on the phone. Eddie didn't get the name of the place and asked her to repeat it. "Whale and Bull," she told him, "W, H, A, L, E . . ." He said quickly, "Patty, I didn't think it was W, A, I, L."

The damndest things seem to happen to jazz musicians. Ask Johnny Frosk, a fine trumpet player I worked with in a Goodman band. Johnny had a serious problem with a moose.

   This was in 1954 or 1955 when he had just left some band and was going to join Tommy Dorsey in Seattle. Since he had a week before he was to be there, he decided to visit his mother, who lived in central Canada, on the drive to Washington state. On the way, one night in Canada on a two-lane road, Johnny and his Plymouth encountered a large moose standing on the road. There wasn't enough room to get around him, so Johnny started to honk the horn. The moose didn't like that. That moose charged directly at the Plymouth and smashed into the front of the car. As the moose pulled his head out, the car radiator and grill came out, too, attached to his horns. Johnny swears that the radiator and the grill were still hanging on the moose's horns when the moose ran off into the woods.

"My God, I was terrified," Frosk told me. He sat there in what was left of his car in what he figured was the middle of nowhere until daylight when a truck driver kindly towed him to a garage. The garage mechanic informed him it would take several days to repair the car—"that moose destroyed it," John said—and John traded it for a used car to complete his trip. He hasn't honked his horn at a moose since.

A friend of mine, Arnold Stone, was a college drummer who became a dentist and one of his patients was in real estate and sold apartment build- ings. The patient had sold one building to the late Lennie Hayton, the conductor and composer who married beautiful Lena Horne. When Lennie was a potential customer, the real estate man entertained Lennie on occasion and was playing golf with him one day. Strolling down the fairway, he asked Hayton if one encounters trouble when you marry a woman of another race. "Well," said Lennie, "the only trouble I had was with Lena's mother. She wouldn't come to our wedding because I'm Jewish."

Al Porcino, first trumpet player, has played in name bands led by Louis Prima, Gene Krupa, Tommy Dorsey, Jerry Wald, Georgie Auld, Stan Kenton, Chubby Jackson, Woody Herman, Pete Rugolo, Count Basie, Eliot Lawrence, Terry Gibbs, Med Flory, and others no doubt. I hadn't seen him for a long time when I spotted him getting into an elevator one day. I yelled, "Hey, Al, how are you?" He smiled, straightened his tie, and replied, "Still the best!"

I loved the way Cy Walter played. He epitomized the whole East Side. In his final years, he had cancer of the jaw. It just kept eating his jaw away. I was working a job in Falmouth, Massachusetts, in 1953 after Goodman got sick and his band disbanded, and on a night off I went over to hear Cy a few miles away at Wood's Hole. Cy was all dolled up in his tuxedo, as usual. An older woman came over to the piano and said, "Oh, I can tell you have studied classical music. Can you play *Clair de Lune?*" Cy said, "Oh, sure," and immediately started into it. Halfway through, he lost track, looked at me, winked, and faked it out pretty well. He wound up with an MGM orchestra flourish. The woman loved it. He leaned toward me and said, "That was the Hollywood version."

9

RHYTHM GUITAR, A DYING ART

My kind of guitar playing is uncommon in jazz today. In fact, it's been uncommon for many years. I play rhythm guitar. There is no electronic boom or buzz. My guitar sound comes from the guitar, not from an amp.

You won't find much, if anything, about the great rhythm guitar players in the many books by jazz critics and historians. And because of the nature of jazz now, the very sound of the rhythm guitar as it once was and ought to be is rarely heard.

As I said during an interview with book colleague Tom Scanlan for a 1965 *Down Beat* essay entitled "The Tough Straight Art": "If you play straight guitar into a microphone, it still sounds like a guitar. But the pickup on an amplified guitar doesn't pick up the sounds of notes. It picks up vibrations of the strings and transmits them through an electronic field that makes little bleeps of them. What you get is a round *oo-oo-oo-oo* sound. Those who use an amplified guitar turn buttons constantly to get the least disagreeable sound possible. But it's all phony. The sound isn't crisp. The sound isn't true. The difference between a good rhythm section and a great one is the guitar. With a good rhythm guitar, you don't get those thudding sounds. I like to think the bass fiddle is the left hand on the piano and the guitar is the right hand."

Freddie Green told me that Allan Reuss straightened out his rhythm work when he was first working with Count Basie, shortly before I went to Allan for help when I was twenty years old and playing with the Bradley-McKinley band. It may surprise some people to know that Green played only three or four strings most of the time. Like me, Freddie followed Allan's rule to avoid use of the first string—the top E—because it's too twangy. Freddie preferred the deep sounds and no one played those deep sounds as well as Freddie did.

For many years Freddie used a Stromberg, a deep-sounding guitar made by Charles Stromberg and then by his son Elmer in Boston until 1955, when Elmer died. When Freddie's Stromberg was beyond repair, the Gretsch company built a guitar for him to the same specifications as the Stromberg and it sounded wonderful. I have a Gibson Super 400 that is something like a Stromberg but prefer the Gibson L-5, which has sharp cutting power and, if desired, you can almost get a snare drum sound out of it. I think it's the greatest rhythm guitar ever made. Introduced by Gibson in 1924, the L-5 was, I believe, the first cello-bodied guitar with sound holes in the classical style.

I haven't heard Reuss play for many years and he'd be in his mid-seventies now. I do know that twenty years or so ago, while playing background music for "I Spy," "Mickey Mouse Club," and other TV shows, he was using a flattop guitar rather than his trusty f-hole guitar. I'd like to hear Reuss in a good band again playing rhythm, although I don't know that he could do it the way he once did since he's been playing soft, easy guitar for many years, and he is older now. When I was young, however, Reuss was the best in the business. All of us in rhythm guitar chairs tried our best but none of us could match Allan Reuss. I think he is the best rhythm guitar player there ever was. And as I said in the first chapter of this book, I'll always be grateful to Allan for the valuable lessons he gave me.

I had a high regard for John Hammond's taste in music, but I was startled to read his comments about Reuss in the 1977 Hammond autobiography, *John Hammond On Record.* He noted "the kind of guitar Benny Goodman liked, the stiff, chugging rhythm guitar exemplified by George Van Eps and Allan Reuss . . ." (I'm with Benny!) and later in reference to the organization of Benny's 1953 band, Hammond wrote, "Benny wanted Allan Reuss on guitar, happily we got Steve Jordan." Well, I certainly understand why Benny wanted Allan, who couldn't make it because he was under contract to the studios in L.A. Of course, I was pleased he couldn't make it. If he had, I probably never would have met and played with Benny Goodman.

Electric guitar soloists have received most of the attention and most of the money in recent years, but few of them can even begin to play rhythm guitar properly. Those who can play rhythm properly have been forgotten, even by jazz historians, and they shouldn't be.

In addition to Reuss, there were several who worked with Goodman before

I did who belong in any book involving big band jazz. Benny Heller, a tiny guy who followed Reuss in the Goodman band and left Benny to go with Harry James when Harry left the clarinetist to begin his own band, was certainly a fine player. He's now selling Gretsch instruments and living in the Washington area. Mike Bryan, a good friend of Georgie Auld's, was another. Bryan was the rhythm man in Benny's band in the early 1940s, when Charlie Christian was electrifying the jazz world with his amplified, single-string guitar solos with the Goodman Sextet. Mike could play with that real tight snap that Benny liked. He could make his arm go around in a circle just playing straight four, no accent. (I played straight four for a long time but I started listening to Freddie Green playing with an accent and began to play that way, too.) Another Goodman guitarist (and Artie Shaw guitarist as well) who impressed me was Pittsburgh's Tommy Morganelli, who became Tommy Morgan. After he returned from the war in the mid-1940s, he played in New York for only a short while before deciding to quit the whole rat race and go back home to Pittsburgh where he joined the police force, playing only Friday and Saturday night jobs. This amazed me at the time, because Tommy was a fine, versatile player able to work with anybody.

Barry Galbraith and Turk Van Lake are two others not to be overlooked in any list of top rhythm men. Barry, who does fancy solo work, too, is still busy in the business. But Turk, the last I heard, is more or less out of music now, doing Lord only knows what and living on Staten Island. Some may remember that Turk made the trip to Russia with Goodman in 1962. I know that Turk enjoyed that tour in more ways than one because he is of Armenian descent (his real name is Vanig Hovsepian) and during that tour, when the band was in Tiflis, in the south of Russia, Turk's aunt came with her son from Armenia to see her nephew Turk for the first time. Though born in Boston, his family comes from the Lake Van region of what was once Armenia but is now part of Turkey, according to George Avakian, who is also of Armenian descent. This may sound as if it all had something to do with how Vanig Hovsepian became Turk Van Lake, but the explanation is simpler. Staten Island was spelled Staaten when the Dutch had New York and Turk just decided to have a Dutch name—Van Lake.

There are a number of other rhythm players who must be mentioned: The late Carl Kress, of whom Paul Whiteman said, "He's not fancy, just terrific!"; Sam Herman, now in his own music copying business, who worked with Benny Goodman and Tommy Dorsey and who shares honors with Turk Van Lake in duplicating Freddie Green's sound; Bucky Pizzarelli, also a fine soloist, who played great rhythm for Goodman and Sauter-Finegan; Mundell Lowe, an excellent soloist, too, who has worked with many top players and has been seen with Goodman and with the Merv Griffin TV band; Herb Ellis, whose terrific rhythm work with Oscar Peterson should never be forgotten, although he is most widely known for his exciting, Christian-inspired solo work; and Freddie Guy, Duke Ellington's banjo player in the 1920s who switched to guitar in the 1930s and whose sound was important *inside* the great Ellington orchestra even if he could not always be heard out front. It ought to be remembered, too, that when Freddie left Ellington in 1947, the Duke never hired another guitar player for his band. Another player who should be included here is Marty Grosz, one of the few in jazz helping to keep the very sound of unamplified guitar alive today.

Rhythm guitar jobs became scarce after World War II when big bands became scarce. Some of the rhythm players learned to read melody and switched to electric guitar, emulating Charlie Christian (though Charlie could not read melody) and his many followers. Others went into studio work. Some just quit the music business. A few, like me, managed to hang in there.

When the big band business began to fade away, the first guy that band-leaders would drop was the guitar player. Next came the third or fourth trombone player, then the fifth saxophone. A rhythm section is not a real rhythm section without a rhythm guitar and many bandleaders were well aware of that fact, but there was only so much money available and ends had to be met. Some bands used rhythm guitar on recordings but not on the road. Woody Herman did this for a while. So did Harry James. Count Basie kept the rhythm guitar (namely Freddie Green) and Benny Goodman always had a rhythm guitar in his off-and-on big band revivals. But Basie and Goodman were exceptions to the rule.

My feeling is that rhythm guitar is not about to return to the big band scene today, what there is of it, simply because there is not enough money around. Also, good rhythm players are hard to find now, especially younger ones. Young guitar players concentrate on solo work, few of them know how to voice chords properly, and there is no demand that they learn how.

In a jazz band today you will often hear a guitarist, hired for his single string solo work, trying to play rhythm on an amplified guitar. It doesn't work. To my mind, neither a bass nor a guitar should be amplified, even in a big, loud band. And to those who say that without amplification you can't always hear the bass and guitar, I say fine, because you are not supposed to hear them all the time. When a band comes down to a certain volume, they will be heard. Contrasting sound, contrasting volumes, is what makes big band jazz fascinating. A big band constantly at the same volume is a bore. Goodman always understood this and Basie always understood this. There is too much amp, amp, amp in big band jazz today. One reason the Basie band stood out so much was because Basie knew that a band must be able to play softly so that its loud passages would have wallop.

Rhythm guitar players are a dying breed of cat now and most people in the music business couldn't care less. You can't even find a tortoise-shell pick any more, only plastic ones that are no damn good. It's hard to find the proper kind of Gibson strings, too. I called the Gibson factory a few years ago and told them I wanted to give them a small order. I wanted to buy $100 worth of Gibson bronze strings. I was told that was "an awfully small order, and besides we're going to discontinue making them soon." I told the Gibson man I have two Gibson L-5s and a Gibson Super 400 and I asked him if the Gibson bronze strings I wanted were not specifically designed for those models. He said they were and agreed with me that other strings didn't sound nearly as good on these particular f-hole guitars. I said, "Well, each of my three Gibson guitars has a lifetime guarantee, I am still alive, and you are going to have to supply strings for those instruments." So he sent me the small order, so many D strings, so many G strings, different amounts for each of the six strings, all singles. It was about the only way I could get the Gibson strings I need.

In Syracuse in 1976, where I spent the summer with the Jack Maheu band, there was a music store that claimed to have a complete line of all guitar strings including Gibson strings. But when I went in to pick up some Gibson bronze strings, they had none. They had only lightweight mona steel and electric strings. It's that way across the nation now, I'm sure. There's not enough call for bronze strings and Gibson no longer makes them. Everything is designed for the electric guitar today, from those highly flexible picks, the kind mandolin players used to use, to flatwound electric strings.

And the new acoustic f-hole guitars are not to be compared to the old ones in the quality of wood, craftsmanship, or tone. A few years ago it took a year to get a Gibson L-5 or Super 400 and I'm told the newer ones have plywood backs, not maple backs. That's very discouraging. And a new L-5 costs well over $1,000. An L-5 I bought for about $300 before World War II is now worth at least $3,000. Another L-5 I bought in 1960 cost $650 and is infinitely superior to the $1,800 models produced today. A new Super 400 (so named because it was priced at $400 when it first came out in 1934) probably runs around $2,000 and I'm sure it would be decidedly inferior to my aging model. In fact, I heard you can't even order one now. Apparently, they won't make one for any price. John D'Aguisto, on Long Island, makes good rhythm guitars similar to the Gibson L-5 and Super 400 but a few years ago I was told he had a three-year waiting list and each of his guitars costs about $2,000. Maybe much more than that by now. To my knowledge, no one else in the United States is making such a guitar.

This all sounds discouraging for anyone in the rhythm guitar business, but I still have my L-5s in working condition and enough strings to get by, I think. It reminds me of a Mark Twain remark that came after a Wagnerian concert.

"How did you like Wagner?" Twain was asked.

"To tell you the truth," Twain replied, "it's not as bad as it sounds."

10

STILL PLAYING

For many jazz musicians today, it's good that money isn't everything because gigs are sometimes scarce, if you favor understatement. In Washington, and I'm sure it's true in other cities, some of the best musicians survive with daytime jobs. I had one myself at one time, selling men's clothes. But I'm not complaining. I have a wonderful wife (Pat and I will be celebrating our twenty-eighth anniversary in 1991), and a wonderful daughter, Julie. Also, I seem to have won my battle with throat cancer, mentioned earlier, making me one of the lucky ones. And now that I'm over seventy I don't have to give Uncle Sam some of my Social Security money back!

During the past fifteen years or so, steady gigs have been uncommon, but there have been some memorable times on the bandstand. For example:

I played with what is called a "traditional" jazz band during the summer of 1976. It was my first experience with such a group. Once in a while we'd play something as modern as *Muskrat Ramble*. We specialized in tunes such as *The Oriental Strut* which was written in 1918 for the Oriental Theater in Chicago by banjo player Johnny St. Cyr.

This band was billed as Jack Maheu and the Salt City Six (Plus One). I was the "one." I had played and recorded with Jack at the Manassas Jazz Festival. He had always used a banjo in his band before but, after hearing me, he started to dig the guitar sound. I worked with him for a month in Rochester and another month in Syracuse.

This was not a dull, dreary Dixieland band, playing too much slow music too often. This band played with lots of pepper. Maheu is a terrific clarinet player, with a technique that brings Artie Shaw to mind. The pianist, Don

Coates, from Vermont, was excellent, too. He was inspired by Don Ewell, who certainly played traditional jazz piano as well as anyone. The drummer, Charlie Cameron, was also awfully good. He knew precisely when to do what with the sticks in every tune we played. The trombone player was Will Alger, who was under fifty but looked older. He was bald, with a big Italian moustache, and he sang old tunes beautifully. Maheu and Alger formed the band in 1952 in Syracuse (thus the Salt City name) when both were in their twenties. When other musicians their age were digging Dizzy, Kenton, or the Herman Herd, they were flipping over Jelly Roll Morton and his contemporaries.

The bass player was an old friend, Billy Goodall, who had worked with George Shearing, Charlie Barnet, and Tommy Dorsey. He had no trouble fitting in with a "trad" band, but some of the tunes we played were as new to him as they were to me. We rehearsed one afternoon a week just to get a new tune—that is, another *old* "new" tune—down right. One afternoon as we were rehearsing, when the club was closed, the bartender was getting his stuff set up and telling a young waiter, a college kid, to move a bar stool. The kid looked around, perplexed. Billy yelled to the youngster: "Hey, man, don't you know what a bar stool is? Davy Crockett stepped in one of those!"

Working with Maheu and the Salt City Six added up to one of the most pleasant summers I've ever spent. Playing traditional jazz their way was fun. I wasn't asked back the following summer because of money. He could afford only the same amount of cash for the band and, instead of guitar, he had a girl who could sing and look pretty. That's the way it goes and that kind of personnel switch is traditional. Traditionally commercial, you might say. I understand, naturally, and I still love Jack.

In 1977, I worked a regular gig with an excellent cocktail lounge pianist, Catherine Chrishon, a lovely, elegant young woman. She is a popular performer in Washington and deserves to be. But she is not a jazz player and working with her reminded me that jazz players and cocktail lounge pianists, no matter how good, differ and that some musicians don't quite understand what jazz is all about. Although she has a master's degree in music and can play in any key you want, she has an affinity for the key of C. When we'd begin our first set, I'd often kid her, "well, here we go, another evening in C!" And I was constantly surprised at the standards she didn't know. She didn't know *Just One of Those Things,* for example. But having worked with some fine jazz players including Keter Betts since then, Catherine is certainly a much better player today than she was fifteen years ago.

One night, in 1977, as she was flying over the keyboard sounding like a symphony orchestra, she turned to me and said, "Play the next chorus." I got in about four bars, and then she started accompanying, accompanying, accompanying, and soon my solo was a piano solo. Between sets, I had to explain that I don't play single notes, I play chords, and I have the whole thing right there in my left hand. I asked her, that when I solo, to either comp or stop playing completely. I tried to teach her that she should stick to the basic chord changes, and not reharmonize. Anyone with an ear as good as she has can reharmonize all night but that doesn't have anything to do with jazz. As Teddy Wilson once said, "When the background gets too complex, it kills the solo. To me, even the Charlie Parker–like soloists would sound much better if they had simpler harmonic backgrounds, then their own harmonic thinking would come over better."

To play jazz, you use the basic chord changes and then see how much you've got in your head to work pretty melodic sounds in against those basic changes. When a trumpet player takes a solo in a big band, the chords the band is going to play are written on his chart so he knows where he's going. He doesn't just ad lib.

In the Blues Alley chapter, I mentioned that the first standout bass player I met after coming to Washington in 1959 was Keter Betts. The next Washington bass player of true quality I met was Perry Van Vedder, better known as Van Perry. He does not play like Keter. He has a different approach. His rhythm playing is more of a "thud," similar to the sound of Walter Page. And his ear for harmony and sense of perfect time puts him in the top category. In short, he swings. Van also has a fine sense of humor. To wit:

We were playing a trio gig with Catherine Chrishon, and during one set, Van said, "I'll sing one. Make it *Here's That Rainy Day* in E-flat."

Catherine played a pretty piano introduction, Van started to sing and found that she had gone into *Stormy Weather.* He stopped singing and corrected her. She laughed and said, "Let's start again." Another nice intro by Catherine followed and Van started singing again. But this time she went into *A Foggy Day.* Van stopped, smiled and said, "Never mind. I can't sing in this kind of weather!"

A few years ago Tommy Gwaltney hired Van and me to play some unobtrusive incidental music for a banker's convention at the Woodlawn Plantation near Mount Vernon. The house is a southern mansion that George Washington had built as a wedding present for his stepdaughter. The whole place was gorgeous.

We played during the cocktail party and discovered a few music lovers.

A couple from Detroit asked about requests and we said okay. But they couldn't decide right away what they wanted to hear. So the woman turned to Van and asked, "Well, what do these lovely surroundings prompt you to do?"

Van, who is black, gave her his big smile and said, "Pick cotton, ma'am!"

For about five years during the late 1980s, I worked regularly with drummer Brooks Tegler's Hot Jazz group. Since Hot Jazz sounds like the name of a Dixieland or trad band, perhaps the band should be called Hot Swing. We played Goodman Sextet pieces such as *A Smo-o-o-oth One, Slipped Disc, Gone With What Wind?, Soft Winds, Benny's Bugle,* and *Airmail Special.* Also, Artie Shaw Gramercy Five pieces such as *Scuttlebutt, Summit Ridge Drive, The Sad Sack,* and *Mysterioso.* Plus trickery arrangements that Charlie Shavers did for the John Kirby group. Is there any other band in the nation playing this wonderful music of the 1930s and 1940s now?

I think Gene Krupa would have enjoyed the drumming of Brooks Tegler, who has modeled his playing on Krupa's mastery of sticks and brushes. Brooks won't even use plastic drumheads. Only skin. Lord knows where he gets them. In his basement music room, in a glass display case under a blue light, he has a complete set of Gene Krupa drums, Slingerland Radio Kings dating from the early 1940s. All the drumheads are signed by Gene. He also has a full set of Gene's cymbals from the 1950s. Brooks was inspired by Krupa when he saw him as a kid, and at times he really does sound like Gene.

Tegler's group has some different players now, but in 1989, when I was still working with the band, it included trumpet player Clyde Hunt, a terrific soloist who did just about all of the writing for the group, and John Cocuzzi, who has got to be one of the swingingest young vibes players in the country. Besides having a marvelous ear for harmony, John has fire, enthusiasm, and speed with the mallets. He also plays fine piano. Our other pianist, Sid Keithley, was a World War II fighter pilot who has since been fighting the piano and winning always. We also had Ron Hockett, a truly polished clarinetist who doubles on tenor and alto saxes. Two bass players split our gigs. Terry Benton is a powerhouse in the tradition of Walter Page. Sal DeRaffele has good time, a good choice of color tones, good solos, and a good outlook in that he doesn't realize he's as good as he is.

Gary Gregg was with the band when I first joined it. Gary was forty-seven in 1990, so he can't recall the swing era of jazz, but on clarinet he is Goodmanesque, and on tenor sax he certainly plays more like Charlie Ventura, Buddy Tate, and other swing era stars than most all reed men his age do. Like Scott Hamilton, a more widely known tenorman who is younger than Gary, he plays as if the bop revolution and John Coltrane's "sheets of sound" never happened. When I first heard Gary he was a Dixieland player. By the time I played with him, he had listened to a lot of Benny Goodman and great swing tenor players like Lester Young. And it showed. Gary is one of those Washington musicians with a good daytime government job.

In 1987 I worked a gig at Washington's National Press Club with tenor saxophonist Benny Waters, who was with Charlie Johnson in the 1920s and Fletcher Henderson and Jimmie Lunceford in the 1930s. Benny was then eighty-five years old! He looked, moved, talked and played twenty-five years younger than that. Discussing his days with Lunceford, who had a great band that was also known as the best-dressed band, Benny said that the band traveled with seven different uniforms, including different shirts, socks, shoes, and ties for each uniform. The suits were sent in wardrobe trunks ahead of the band. "And one afternoon I caught hell from Jimmie because I came on stage with the wrong socks!" Times have changed. Ever notice how most bands dress today?

And who says jazz is only a young man's game? Milt Hinton, Lionel Hampton, Benny Carter, and Doc Cheatham still sound great and all are over eighty. The late Bud Freeman, at eighty-two, sounded fine at the 1988 Manassas Jazz Festival. And bass player Johnny Williams, who worked with Louis Armstrong, Coleman Hawkins, and Teddy Wilson, certainly did not sound or look eighty-one years old when I worked with him at a 1989 tribute to Eddie Condon. Also on that gig was drummer Johnny Blowers, then seventy-eight, who played with the Condon gang over fifty years ago. Johnny still lays down a powerful beat with taste and wallop.

So I'm hanging in there. In addition to other gigs here and there, in 1990 I led a trio and quartet on a once-a-week schedule, using Washington jazz players such as John Jensen, standout trombonist with the U.S. Navy's orchestra, The Commodores; tenor man Al Seibert, who played with Woody Herman and whose big sound reminds me of Coleman Hawkins; and former "Hot Jazz" colleagues John Cocuzzi, Sid Keithley, and Terry Benton.

I'm not a "big name" known to the so-called man on the street, but I do discover from time to time that I'm not unknown in some unexpected places. When a sextet of Russian jazz musicians visited Washington about two years ago, I was introduced to one who said, "Steve Jordan! Legendary guitar player!"

In Australia, Bruce Clarke runs a guitar studio with well over 100 students in Victoria's East Malvern. He is a top-grade jazz guitarist and has played duets with Herb Ellis when Herb has been on tour there (you've got to be a fine player to handle duets with Herb). Herb Mecking, another guitar player, had introduced me to Clarke by mail. Clarke has been sending me fascinating tapes of work by him, his teachers, and his students, including a strikingly different one that has one rhythm player and four other guitarists playing single string lines in harmony together, sounding like a saxophone section does. Clarke knows my playing only by recordings, but on one of his tapes he tells me, "If I never meet you or never hear you play again, I'll always say you are the very best rhythm guitar player there ever was." True or not, that remark really cheered me up.

And in 1991 I received a fan letter from Kobe, Japan. It said, in part: "I am very enjoying your cassette tapes everyday. I like the sound of acoustic guitar (non amp). . . . Of course, I love your beautiful fine play for a long time. I play by Gibson, 1947. I like the sound of Gibson L-5."

So I said one day to my trumpet playing friend Clyde Hunt: "How come I'm legendary in Russia, 'my beautiful fine play' is loved in Japan, I have fans in Australia, and I can't get a steady gig in Alexandria, Virginia?"

Clyde replied quickly: "*That* should tell you something about Alexandria, Virginia."

Most all Alexandria clubs do prefer rock bands, country bands, skiffle bands, folk groups, and assorted amateur musicians to jazz players. And that's true of many cities now, I'm sure.

I am sometimes asked about jazz critics. There are good ones and bad ones, I think, and I do believe that critics should separate fact from opinion. For example, when a critic baldly writes that Benny Goodman bands had no "first-rate" tenor sax players, he is actually saying that Vido Musso, Bud Freeman, Jerry Jerome, Babe Russin, Georgie Auld, Budd Johnson, and Zoot Sims were not first rate. That is surely not fact. That is opinion, curious opinion I'd say, which tells us more about the writer than the players he is knocking. Critics should use the phrase "in my opinion" more often.

Musicians tend to think differently than critics. I'm sure some self-appointed authorities would be surprised to learn that Vic Dickenson's favorite trumpet player was Harry James. Vic once detailed for me the reasons why, with great praise for James, one of many famous players some prominent critics habitually put down.

And I do think that musicians from the swing era have not received proper acclaim in recent years. I could offer a number of jazz history books as proof.

It has been suggested that jazz enthusiasts are divided into two groups of people, those who think jazz all but died with Baby Dodds and Bix Beiderbecke and those who think jazz started with Stan Kenton or Charlie Parker and Dizzy Gillespie. John Hammond made this point in an interview with Lillian Ross published in the *New Yorker* years ago. What about the musicians in between? John mentioned Buck Clayton, Jo Jones, Walter Page, and me as examples.

After all, the real golden age of jazz, when there were many great players around and all able to get work, too, was the swing era, the late 1930s and early 1940s. Perhaps I feel this way because I am of that generation. But to my mind, when the big bands were cooking, when 52nd Street meant music, was when it was really happening. There were dozens, maybe hundreds of exciting young players then. Don't tell me that's true today.

It's a completely different musical world now. To my generation, popular music meant Irving Berlin, Cole Porter, George Gershwin. For today's generation, popular music means rock performers, and I still find it hard to believe that some famous rock people actually burn guitars on stage.

Those of us who grew up in the 1930s sometimes forget that later generations know little about jazz and popular music as it was before the advent of rock.

A few years ago I was on my apartment balcony one afternoon playing guitar. A bright young lady on the next balcony, visibly impressed, said, "Oh, Mr. Jordan, I didn't know you could play guitar so well. Have you ever played professionally?"

"Oh, yes, still do," I said, adding, "I worked with Benny Goodman for four years."

"Benny Goodman," she said with a quizzical look. "I *think* I've heard of him."

So, the big bands are gone, jazz clubs and jazz jobs are scarce, and most young people don't know who Benny Goodman was. But I intend to keep on playing as long as it remains fun. As Mark Twain said, "Work is what you do when you'd rather be doing something else," and in that sense music usually hasn't been work for me. It's been fun.

And although television programmers, most record company executives, and most clubowners apparently don't agree, I think there's still an audience out there looking for good jazz.

One more thing. Despite occasional grumbling about the pronouncements of some critics, let it be known that I learned a long time ago that musicians aren't the only ones who know about music.

Over forty years ago, while at home in Flushing, Long Island, after a road tour, I was having a beer with a guy named Tony Rumifero, who was about sixty years old, smoked a corncob pipe, and earned his living running a small cement mixer for a construction firm on Long Island. He knew I was a musician and half-Italian, and he asked me if I liked opera. "Oh, yes," I said, "and Puccini is wonderful." I raved on about *Madame Butterfly* and *La Bohème*.

"Puccini issa vedy gooda," Tony said, "but the besta opp'ida issa *La Lucia di Lammermoor.* You go homma tonight and eska you gramma what's the besta opp'ida. She'sa know."

He didn't know my grandmother but knew she had come from Italy.

So I went home and there was grandma, about eighty years old, knitting as usual. "Hey, grandma," I asked point blank, "what's the best opera?"

She looked up from her knitting, shrugged, and said, "*La Lucia*, what else?"

SELECTED DISCOGRAPHY

Recordings by Steve Jordan are listed in chronological order, dating from 1940 to 1990, by group leader's name. LP or cassette title, if there is one, follows in parentheses. The Will Bradley and Boyd Raeburn albums are reissues of what were originally 78 rpm recordings. Many of the LPs listed below can still be found in stores specializing in jazz, some are available by mail from jazz record dealers, and it is always possible that some of this music will be reissued on cassettes or CDs.

Partly because of the 1942–44 recording ban, and mainly because the bands did not happen to be in recording studios when Jordan was with them, he did not record with bands led by Artie Shaw, Teddy Powell, Bob Chester, Freddie Slack, Glen Gray, and Stan Kenton. Although Boyd Raeburn made other recordings, including two sessions listed here, the large, innovative Raeburn band that Jordan was with on the road in 1947–48 was not recorded.

Some unissued Benny Goodman tapes, with Jordan on guitar, including concert performances in Bangkok and Tokyo in December, 1956, and January, 1957, are listed in the superb discography *Benny Goodman, Listen to His Legacy* by D. Russell Connor. Other unissued music by Goodman with Jordan on guitar is to be found in that 1988 book and in its earlier version, *BG on the Record* by Connor and Warren Hicks, published in 1969.

Several albums and two cassettes in this discography include recordings without Jordan, but only tracks or cuts on these albums and cassettes with Jordan on guitar are listed.

For the convenience of the reader, record company names are not abbreviated. Instrument abbreviations are: tp (trumpet), tb (trombone), ts (tenor sax), as (alto sax), bs (baritone sax), cl (clarinet), p (piano), g (guitar), eg (electric guitar), b (bass), d (drums), voc (vocals), vib (vibes), vtb (valve trombone), cor (cornet), bj (banjo).

Will Bradley Orchestra   (1939–41, Featuring Ray McKinley, vol. 1)
                                                                Bandstand BS-1
January 31, 1940 to January 21, 1941 (Reissued ca. 1977)
[Note: Jordan is not on the band's first five recordings, also reissued here. Jordan's
first recording session with Bradley was January 31, 1940.]

Will Bradley, Jim Emert, Bill Corti, tb; Steve Lipkins, Joe Wiedman, Al Mitchell,
tp; Art Mendelsohn, Joe Huffman, Nick Ciazza (Peanuts Hucko on some tracks),
Sam Sachelle, saxes; Freddie Slack, p; Steve Jordan, g; Doc Goldberg, b; Ray
McKinley, d, voc; Louise Tobin, voc.

I Get a Kick Out of Corn / Scramble Two / In a Spanish Town / Deed I Do /
Lonesome Road / Five O'Clock Whistle / Three Ring Ragout / This Little Icky
Went to Town / Southpaw Serenade

Will Bradley Orchestra   (1939–41, vol. 2)
                                                                Bandstand 7110
January 21, 1941 to January 8, 1942 (Reissued ca. 1977)

Will Bradley, Jim Emert, Bill Corti (Bill Ruppersburg) tb; Steve Lipkins, Joe
Wiedman, Al Mitchell (Alec Fila, Lee Castaldo, Ralph Muzzillo, Jimmy Grimes,
Tommy Dicarlo, Ralph Snyder, Dick Haas, Pete Candoli, Tony Faso) tp; Peanuts
Hucko, Art Mendelsohn, Jo Huffman, Sam Sachelle (Mahlon Clark, Johnny Van
Epps, John Mays, Les Robinson, Pete Mondello, Art Rollini, Larry Mollinelli,
George Koenig) saxes; Freddie Slack (Bob Holt, Billy Maxted) p; Steve Jordan, g;
Doc Goldberg (Felix Giobbe) b; Ray McKinley, d, voc; Terry Allen, Lynn
Gardner, voc.

Fascination / Quicksilver / Bounce Me, Brother, With a Solid Four / Tea for
Two / A City Called Heaven / Request for a Rhumba / I Think of You / The
Three B's / When You and I Were Young, Maggie / It's Square, But It Rocks /
Jack and Jill / April in Paris / In the Hall of the Mountain King / Basin Street
Boogie / All That Meat and No Potatoes / Fry Me, Cookie, With a Can of Lard

Will Bradley-Ray McKinley   (Rock-a-Bye the Boogie)
                                                                Bandstand 7112
March 13, 1940 to June 23, 1941
(Reissued ca. 1977)

Will Bradley, Jim Emert, Bill Corti, tb; Joe Wiedman, Steve Lipkins, Herbie Dell
(Al Mitchell, Lee Castaldo, Alec Fila) tp; Jo Huffman, Art Mendelsohn, Peanuts
Hucko, Sam Sachelle (Nick Ciazza, Mahlon Clark, Johnny Hayes) saxes; Freddie
Slack (Bob Holt, Billy Maxted), p; Steve Jordan, g; Felix Giobbe (Doc Goldberg) b;
Ray McKinley, d, voc; Jimmy Valentine, Terry Allen, voc.

Beat Me Daddy, Eight to the Bar / O Sole Mio / Basin Street Boogie / Stardust / Rhumboogie / In the Land of the Sky Blue Water / Scrub Me, Mama, With a Boogie Beat / Boogie Woogie Conga / Dark Eyes / Chicken Gumboogie / Booglie Wooglie Piggy / Bugles in the Sky / I Boogied When I Should Have Woogied / Rock-a-Bye the Boogie

Boyd Raeburn Orchestra

(Boyd Meets Stravinsky)
Savoy MG-12040

1945 (Reissued ca. 1964) All arrangements by George Handy

Dizzy Gillespie, Benny Harris, Tommy Allison, Stan Fishelson, tp; Trummy Young, Ollie Wilson, Jack Carmen, Walt Robertson, tb; Johnny Bothwell, Hal McKusick, as; Joe Magro, Al Cohn, ts; Serge Chaloff, bs; Ike Carpenter, p; Steve Jordan, g; Oscar Pettiford, b; Shelly Manne, d.

Interlude (Night in Tunisia) / Summertime / March of the Boyds

Dale Pierce, Tommy Allison, Carl Berg, Allan Jeffreys, tp; Jack Carmen, Johnny Mandel, Trummy Young, tb; Johnny Bothwell, Lennie Green, Frank Socolow, Stu Anderson, Hy Mandel, reeds; Ike Carpenter, p; Steve Jordan, g; Joe Beris, b; Irv Kluger, d; Margie Wood, voc.

Blue Prelude / Boyd's Nest / You've Got Me Crying Again

Vic Dickenson

(Showcase, vol. 1)
Vanguard VRS-8001

December 29, 1953

Vic Dickenson, tb; Ruby Braff, tp; Edmond Hall, cl; Sir Charles Thompson, p; Steve Jordan, g; Walter Page, b; Les Erskine, d.

Russian Lullaby / Jeepers Creepers / I Cover the Waterfront / Sir Charles at Home / Keeping' Out of Mischief Now

Vic Dickenson

(Showcase, vol. 2)
Vanguard VRS-8012

Same date and personnel listed above.

Everybody Loves My Baby / When You and I Were Young, Maggie / You Brought a New Kind of Love to Me / Nice Work If You Can Get It

Mel Powell

(Septet)
Vanguard VRS-8004

December 30, 1953

Mel Powell, p; Buck Clayton, tp; Henderson Chambers, tb; Edmond Hall, cl; Steve
Jordan, g; Walter Page, b; James Crawford, d.

'S Wonderful / It's Been So Long / I Must Have That Man / You're Lucky to Me

Buck Clayton   (Jumpin' at the Woodside)
                                                               Columbia CL-701
March 31, 1954

Buck Clayton, Joe Thomas, tp; Urbie Green, Trummy Young, tb; Woody Herman,
cl; Lem Davis, as; Al Cohn, Julian Dash, ts; Jimmy Jones, p; Steve Jordan, g;
Walter Page, b; Jo Jones, d.

Jumpin' at the Woodside / How High the Fi / Blue Moon

Mel Powell   (and His All-Stars)
                                                               Columbia CL-557
April 9, 1954 (Carnegie Hall)

Mel Powell, p; Buck Clayton, Ruby Braff, tp; Urbie Green, Vernon Brown, tb;
Tony Scott, cl; Lem Davis, as; Buddy Tate, ts; Steve Jordan, g; Milt Hinton, b;
Jo Jones, d; Martha Lou Harp, voc.

When Day Is Done / I Found a New Baby / Lighthouse Blues

Buck Clayton and Ruby Braff   (Buck Meets Ruby)
                                                               Vanguard VRS-8008
July 1, 1954

Buck Clayton, Ruby Braff, tp; Benny Morton, tb; Buddy Tate, ts; Jimmy Jones, p;
Steve Jordan, g; Aaron Bell, b; Bobby Donaldson, d.

Kandee / I Can't Get Started / Love Is Just Around the Corner / Just a Groove

Benny Goodman   (B.G. in Hi-Fi)
                                                               Capitol CAP-W656
November 9 and 17, 1954

Benny Goodman, cl; Chris Griffin, Ruby Braff, Bernie Privin, Carl Poole, tp; Will
Bradley, Cutty Cutshall, Vernon Brown, tb; Hymie Schertzer, Paul Ricci, as;
Boomie Richman, Al Klink, ts; Sol Schlinger, bs; Mel Powell, p; Steve Jordan, g;
George Duvivier, b; Bobby Donaldson, d.

Let's Dance / Jumpin' at the Woodside / Stompin' at the Savoy / When I Grow
Too Old to Dream / You Brought a New Kind of Love to Me / Somebody Stole
My Gal / Blue Lou / Sent for You Yesterday (and Here You Come Today) / Big
John Special / Jersey Bounce

November 8, 1954

Benny Goodman, cl; Charlie Shavers, tp; Mel Powell, p; Steve Jordan, g; George Duvivier, b; Bobby Donaldson, d.

Get Happy

Vic Dickenson (Showcase, vol. 3)
Vanguard VRS-8013

November 29, 1954

Vic Dickenson, tb; Ruby Braff, Shad Collins, tp; Edmond Hall, cl; Sir Charles Thompson, p; Steve Jordan, g; Jo Jones, d.

Suspension Blues / Runnin' Wild / Old Fashioned Love

Buck Clayton (All the Cats Join In)
Columbia CL-882

March 5, 1955

Buck Clayton, Billy Butterfield, Ruby Braff, tp; J. C. Higginbotham, tb; Tyree Glenn, tb, vib; Coleman Hawkins, Julian Dash, ts; Ken Kersey, p; Steve Jordan, g; Walter Page, b; Bobby Donaldson, d; Jimmy Rushing, voc.

All the Cats Join In / Don't You Miss Your Baby?

March 15, 1955

Buck Clayton, Ruby Braff, tp; Benny Green, Dicky Harris, tb; Coleman Hawkins, Buddy Tate, ts; Al Waslohn, p; Steve Jordan, g; Milt Hinton, b; Jo Jones, d.

Out of Nowhere / Blue Lou

Sir Charles Thompson (and His Band, Featuring Coleman Hawkins)
Vanguard VRS-8009

1955

Sir Charles Thompson, p; Emmett Berry, tp; Benny Morton, tb; Earl Warren, as; Coleman Hawkins, ts; Steve Jordan, g; Aaron Bell, b; Osie Johnson, d.

It's the Talk of the Town / Fore! / Dynaflow / Under the Sweetheart Tree / Ready for Freddie

Jimmy Rushing, Ada Moore, Buck Clayton (Cat Meets Chick)
Columbia CL-778

August 18, 19, and 23, 1955

Buck Clayton, Emmett Berry, tp; Dicky Wells, tb; Eddie Barefield, cl, as; Budd

Johnson, ts; Willard Brown, ts, bs; Sir Charles Thompson, Ken Kersey, p; Steve Jordan, g; Aaron Bell, Milt Hinton, b; Jo Jones, Osie Johnson, d.

Any Place I Hang My Hat Is Home / Pretty Little Baby / I've Got a Feeling I'm Falling / If I Could Be With You / Ain't She Sweet? / You're My Thrill / Between the Devil and the Deep Blue Sea / Gee, Baby, Ain't I Good to You? / Cool Breeze Woman / I Can't Give You Anything But Love / The Blues / After You've Gone

Benny Goodman   (vol. 1, The Yale University Music Library)
                                                                           CIJ-20142F
September 8, 1955
(not released until 1988)

Benny Goodman, cl; Ruby Braff, tp; Urbie Green, tb; Dave McKenna, p; Steve Jordan, g; Tommy Potter, b; Bobby Donaldson, d.

Soft Lights and Sweet Music

Ruby Braff   (Braff!!!)
                                                                      Epic LN-3377
June 26, 1956

Ruby Braff, tp; Dave McKenna, p; Steve Jordan, g; Buzzy Drootin, d.

Stardust / Blue, Turning Grey Over You / It's Been So Long / How Long Has This Been Going On?

Jimmy Rushing   (The Jazz Odyssey of James Rushing, Esq.)
with Buck Clayton Orchestra   Columbia CL-963
November 8, 1956

Buck Clayton, Ed Lewis, Billy Butterfield, tp; Urbie Green, Dicky Wells, tb; Hilton Jefferson, Rudy Powell, as; Budd Johnson, ts; Hank Jones, p; Steve Jordan, g; Milt Hinton, b; Jo Jones, d; Jimmy Rushing, voc.

Lullaby of Broadway / Old Fashioned Love / Some of These Days

Gene Krupa   (Trio and Sextet, Drum Boogie)
                                                                    Clef MG C-703
Ca. 1956

Charlie Shavers, tp; Willie Smith, as; Teddy Wilson, p; Steve Jordan, g; Israel Crosby, b; Gene Krupa, d.

Capital Idea / Paradise

Ruby Braff

(Hi-Fi Salute to Bunny)
RCA Victor LPM-1510

1957

Ruby Braff, tp; Benny Morton, tb; Pee Wee Russell, cl; Dick Hafer, ts; Nat Pierce, p; Steve Jordan, g; Walter Page, b; Buzzy Drootin, d.

Keep Smiling at Trouble / I Can't Get Started / It's Been So Long / I'm Comin', Virginia / Marie / Downhearted Blues / I Got It Bad / Somebody Else Is Taking My Place

Ruby Braff

(Octet at Newport)
Verve MG V-8241

July 5, 1957 (Newport Jazz Festival)

Ruby Braff, tp; Pee Wee Russell, cl; Sam Margolis, ts; Jimmy Welch, vtb; Nat Pierce, p; Steve Jordan, g; Walter Page, b; Buzzy Drootin, d.

It Don't Mean a Thing (If It Ain't Got That Swing) / These Foolish Things / Oh, Lady Be Good!

Nelson Riddle

(Phil Silvers and Swinging Brass)
Columbia CL-1011

1957

Bernie Glow, Jimmy Maxwell, Charlie Shavers, Dale McMickle, tp; Will Bradley, Warren Covington, Urbie Green, Jack Satterfield, tb; Hymie Schertzer, Sid Cooper, Al Klink, Boomie Richman, Hal Feldman, saxes; Artie Baker, cl; Hank Jones, p; Steve Jordan, g; Frank Carroll, b; Don Lamond, d; Terry Snyder, vib, bongos, chimes.

Hurry Up and Wait / Early Bird / Last Chance / Chow, a Can of Cow and Thou / Two Arms / Scramble / Where'd Everybody Go? / Come as You Are / No Letter Today / The Eagle Screams / Let It Rain, Let it Pour / Lights Out

Tommy Gwaltney

(Plays Great Jazz)
Laurel 163011

1964

Tommy Gwaltney, cl, vib; John Eaton, p; Steve Jordan, g, voc.

Carioca / Satin Doll / Shim-me-sha-wabble / Judy / Heat Wave / Spring Will Be
a Little Late This Year / The Golden Striker / Air Mail Special / Basin Street
Blues / Softly / When Sonny Gets Blue / I Hear Music / I Go for That / That's a
Plenty

Tommy Gwaltney Quartet

(This Is Blues Alley)
Blues Alley 0001

1965 and 1966

Tommy Gwaltney, cl, vib; John Phillips, p; Steve Jordan, g, voc; Keter Betts, b.

Head and Shoulders / Pretty Face / King City Stomp / Winter Weather / Cuban
Episode / Meine Kleines Kätzchen / Old New Orleans Funeral Procession / Bye
Bye Blues / Who Can I Turn To? / Keter's Blues / SHHHHhhhhhhhh!

Jimmy McPartland

(and His All-Stars, On Stage)
Jazzology J-16

May, 1966 (First Manassas Jazz Festival)

Jimmy McPartland, cor; Slide Harris, tb; Tommy Gwaltney, cl; Marian
McPartland, p; Steve Jordan, g; Keter Betts, b; Jake Hanna, d.

Introduction Blues / Muskrat Ramble / Tin Roof Blues / I'm Gonna Sit Right
Down and Write Myself a Letter / That's a Plenty / Royal Garden Blues / I Ain't
Gonna Give Nobody None of My Jelly Roll / Hello, Dolly / When the Saints Go
Marching In

Wild Bill Davison

(Wild Bill at Bull Run)
Jazzology J-30

September, 1966

Wild Bill Davison, cor; Slide Harris, tb; Tommy Gwaltney, cl; John Eaton, p; Steve
Jordan, g; Keter Betts, b; Bertell Knox, d.

Georgia on My Mind / Rosetta / Blue, Turning Grey Over You / Someday,
Sweetheart / I Found a New Baby / Black and Blue / You're Lucky to Me /
Louisiana

Wild Bill Davison

(I'll Be a Friend With Pleasure)
Fat Cat's Jazz FCJ-106

February, 1968

Wild Bill Davison, cor; Herb Gardner, tb; Tommy Gwaltney, cl; John Eaton, p;
Steve Jordan, g; Bill Goodall, b; Jack Connor, d; Johnson (Fat Cat) McRee, voc.

I'll Be a Friend With Pleasure / Do You Know What It Means to Miss New

Orleans? / Who's Sorry Now? / Memphis Blues / The Wreck of the Old '97 /
Call Me Irresponsible / River, Stay Way From My Door / Wang, Wang Blues /
Washington and Lee Swing

Wild Bill Davison

(Lady of the Evening)
Fat Cat's Jazz FCJ-120

April, 1971

Wild Bill Davison, cor; John Eaton, p; Steve Jordan, g; Jack Lesberg, b; Cliff
Leeman, d.

Lady of the Evening / My Honey's Lovin' Arms / Lover, Come Back to Me / New
Orleans / Duet / Thou Swell / But Beautiful / I Can't Get Started / If I Had
You / Coquette

Clancy Hayes

(Mr. Hayes Goes to Washington,
with Tommy Gwaltney and the Blues Alley Cats)
Clanco 814

1972

Clancy Hayes, voc, bj; Tommy Gwaltney, cl, vib; John Phillips, p; Steve Jordan, g;
Billy Taylor, Jr., b; Bertell Knox, d.

Sweet Georgia Brown / St. Louis Blues / Lonesome Road / Tin Roof Blues /
Capital City / Ballin' the Jack / Hindustan / Parsons, Kansas, Blues / Poor
Butterfly / A Trip to Rio / Way Down Yonder in New Orleans

Steve Jordan

(Here Comes Mr. Jordan)
Fat Cat's Jazz 119

March 6 and 20, 1971; May 14, 1972

Steve Jordan, g, voc; Billy Goodall, b.

At Sundown / P.S. I Love You / It Happened in Monterey / Nina Never Knew /
'S Wonderful / Last Night on the Back Porch / Tangerine / Judy / Baubles,
Bangles, and Beads / The Lady's in Love With You / One, Two, Buckle My
Shoe / Steve's Waltz / I Go for That / I See Your Face Before Me / The Coo-Coo
Song / I'm Drinking Again / Honeysuckle Rose / You're Getting to Be a Habit
With Me / You Turned the Tables on Me / Riff-Raff / (I Still Get a Thrill)
Thinking of You

Buddy Tate

(and His Buddies)
Chiaroscuro CR-123

1973

Buddy Tate, Illinois Jacquet, ts; Roy Eldridge, tp; Mary Lou Williams, p; Steve
Jordan, g; Milt Hinton, b; Gus Johnson, d.

Rockaway / Medi-2 / Paris Nights / When I'm Blue / Sunday

Helen Ward

(Song Book, vol. 1)
Lyricon LRI-1001

January 9, March 26–27, June 25, and August 11, 1979

Bucky Pizzarelli, eg, leader; Bernie Privin, Pee Wee Erwin, tp; Ruby Braff, cor;
George Masso, Vic Dickenson, tb; Phil Bodner, cl; Al Cohn, ts; Mickey Crane,
Tony Monte, p; Steve Jordan, g; Warren Chiasson, vib; Milt Hinton, Slam
Stewart, b; Butch Miles, Bobby Rosengarden, d; Helen Ward, voc.

You Can't Pull the Wool Over My Eyes / I've Got the World on a String /
Someone to Watch Over Me / Pennies From Heaven / There'll Be Some Changes
Made / I Thought About You / Goody Goody / Jeepers Creepers / The Glory of
Love / In a Spanish Town / 'S Wonderful / Keepin' Out of Mischief Now / The
Second Time Around / Come Rain or Come Shine

Tommy Gwaltney

(Pee Wee Russell's Land of Jazz, A Memorial Tribute)
Teaspoon S-2981

September 15, 1981

Tommy Gwaltney, cl; George Masso, tb, arranger; Tom Pletcher, cor; Charlie
Harmon, ts, bs; Dill Jones, p; Steve Jordan, g; Bob Haggart, b; Cliff Leeman, d.

Save Your Sorrow for Tomorrow / Crying All Day / Take Me to the Land of
Jazz / Feeling No Pain / I Must Have That Man / Hello, Lola / Friar's Point
Shuffle / Pee Wee's Song / I'm in the Market for You / I Ain't Gonna Give
Nobody None of My Jelly Roll

Ed Polcer

(In the Condon Tradition)
Jazzology J-150

1986 (Manassas Jazz Festival)

Ed Polcer, cor; Bill Allred, tb; John Eaton, p; Steve Jordan, g; Van Perry, b;
Barrett Deems, d.

Nobody's Sweetheart Now / September in the Rain / My Honey's Lovin' Arms /
Shanty in Old Shantytown / Can't We Be Friends? / Put on Your Old Grey
Bonnet

Steve Jordan

(The Intimate Steve Jordan)
B-Flat Music Productions BMP-10001

1987

Steve Jordan, g, voc; Clyde Hunt, tp (on five of the sixteen songs).

I Used to Be Color Blind / There Is No Greater Love / Oh, You Crazy Moon / According to the Moonlight / Once Upon a Midnight / Little Girls / I'm Sorry I Made You Cry / I've Hitched My Wagon to a Star / You're Blasé / Mam'selle / You Brought a New Kind of Love to Me / Fools Rush In / You're Driving Me Crazy / You Can't Pull the Wool Over My Eyes / Ain'tcha Ever Comin' Home, Baby? / Together

Brooks Tegler's Hot Jazz

(Keep 'Em Flying)
Circle CLT-120

July, 1990

(Cassette)

Clyde Hunt, tp; Harry Allen, ts; Ron Hockett, cl; Larry Eanet, p; Steve Jordan, g; Terry Benton, b; Brooks Tegler, d.

Overtime / Coronation Hop / Capital Idea / Cutie Pie

Brooks Tegler's Hot Jazz

(And Not Only That!)
TDC-101

1990

(Cassette)

Clyde Hunt, Chris Badistone, tp; John Jensen, tb; Al Seibert, Harry Allen, ts; Ron Hockett, as; Bruce Swain, as, ts; Jack Moser, bs; Larry Eanet, p; Steve Jordan, g; Steve Abshire, eg; Terry Benton, John Previty, b; Brooks Tegler, d.

And Not Only That! / Early in the Morning

Steve Jordan

(Trio)
B-Flat music Productions BMP-10006

1990

(Cassette)

Steve Jordan, g; John Cocuzzi, vib; Clyde Hunt, tp.

If I Had You / Once In a While / Thou Swell / Someone to Watch Over Me / Jada / Exactly Like You / 'S Wonderful / But Not For Me / There Will Never Be Another You / Solitude / Honeysuckle Rose

INDEX